D1237783

O/:18:2-22

WHAT EVERY AMERICAN NEEDS TO KNOW ABOUT ECONOMICS

Nov. 14, 2018

WHAT EVERY AMERICAN
NEEDS TO KNOW
ABOUT ECONOMICS

TO: Dr. James Willes,
a fellow author,
professor, historian
+ good friend.

David F. Rankin

Copyright © 2018 by David F. Rankin.

Library of Congress Control Number:		2018907570
ISBN:	Hardcover	978-1-9845-3747-8
	Softcover	978-1-9845-3748-5
	eBook	978-1-9845-3749-2

All rights reserved. No part of this book may be reproduced or transmitted in any form or by any means, electronic or mechanical, including photocopying, recording, or by any information storage and retrieval system, without permission in writing from the copyright owner.

Any people depicted in stock imagery provided by Getty Images are models, and such images are being used for illustrative purposes only. Certain stock imagery © Getty Images.

Print information available on the last page.

Rev. date: 09/29/2018

To order additional copies of this book, contact:
Xlibris
1-888-795-4274
www.Xlibris.com
Orders@Xlibris.com
773538

CONTENTS

Dedicated in Honor of:..vii
Acknowledgements..ix
Introduction..xi

Chapter 1 How Many Isms Do You Understand? 1
Chapter 2 Just What Is Capitalism Anyway?..............................6
Chapter 3 We're From the Government, and We Are
           Here to Help You 12
Chapter 4 The Federal Explosion: What Happened?................19
Chapter 5 Incentives Matter, Don't They?................................25
Chapter 6 The Youth Unemployment Maximization Act 30
Chapter 7 Dead-End Jobs: Fact or Fiction? 35
Chapter 8 Taxation without Common Sense 40
Chapter 9 What's So Important about a Central Bank? 50
Chapter 10 Take That, You Dirty Rat!.......................................54
Chapter 11 How Do You Get Economic Growth?......................60
Chapter 12 Have We Discovered the Money Tree?.....................66
Chapter 13 You've Got to Be Kidding! 71
Chapter 14 What Are You Thinking About—Retirement? 80
Chapter 15 The Choice Is Ours!...86

Notes 89
Index..97

DEDICATED IN HONOR OF:

The 56 signers of the Declaration of Independence who, on July 4, 1776, took a bold action that put their lives and those of their families in great peril, for the cause of freedom.

John Adams	Thomas Lynch, Jr.
Samuel Adams	Thomas McKean
Josiah Bartlett	Arthur Middleton
Carter Braxton	Lewis Morris
Charles Carroll	Robert Morris
Samuel Chase	John Morton
Abraham Clark	Thomas Nelson, Jr.
George Clymer	William Paca
William Ellery	Robert Treat Paine
William Floyd	John Penn
Benjamin Franklin	George Read
Elbridge Gerry	Caesar Rodney
Button Gwinnett	George Ross
Lyman Hall	Dr. Benjamin Rush
John Hancock	Edward Rutledge
Benjamin Harrison	Roger Sherman
John Hart	James Smith
Joseph Hewes	Richard Stockton
Thomas Hayward, Jr.	Thomas Stone
William Hooper	George Taylor
Stephen Hopkins	Matthew Thornton
Francis Hopkinson	George Walton
Samuel Huntington	William Whipple

Thomas Jefferson

Francis Lightfoot Lee

Richard Henry Lee

Francis Lewis

Phillip Livingston

William Williams

James Wilson

John Witherspoon

Oliver Wolcott

George Wyth

https://www.archives.gov/files/founding-docs-declaration_signers_gallery_facts.pdf

Acknowledgements

Founded in 1979, the Murphy Lecture at my home campus of Southern Arkansas University gave me the opportunity to rub shoulders with some of the greatest economic and business minds in the country. Mr. Charles Murphy, Jr. of Murphy Oil generously funded a lecture series that made this possible. Thousands of our business students and area citizens have been able to hear and meet the likes of Thomas Sowell, Arthur Laffer, Walter Williams, Stuart Varney and so many national figures. Visiting with these lecturers over the years provided me the opportunity to gain a much-improved perspective on the economic issues of our times. In addition, an opportunity to visit extensively with Milton Friedman provided a rare treat as the result of having one of my students place nationally in the Americanism Educational League economic essay contest.

Both President John Kennedy and President Ronald Reagan impressed on me that sound economic policy can be implemented at the national level. They each proved that national change is actually possible.

The students I have had the privilege to teach over the last fifty years have provided the excitement and satisfaction of watching them grow intellectually and broaden their understanding of the economic world in which we live. The lectures, presentations, and class discussions over the years continue to strengthen my passion to preserve the freedom of the marketplace.

I am grateful to my family who proved a great sounding board for economic ideas around the dinner table. My wife Toni, as well as all three of our children, spent a semester studying macroeconomics under the author. It is amazing the family survived, but it turned out great.

I am also grateful to Governor Mike Huckabee who appointed me as a member, and later chairman, of the Governor's Council of Economic Advisors. This allowed me to be involved with the State Revenue Forecast and other economic issues through the years in his administration as well as the following administrations of both Governor Mike Beebe and Governor Asa Hutchinson.

INTRODUCTION

As a professor of economics and finance—and sometimes a business dean and even a university president, it has become obvious to me that there are a lot of people in America who just don't have much of a clue about how the real world of economics actually works. This continues to be emphasized as important government officials call for higher and higher income taxes, higher minimum wages, burdensome and expensive regulations on business, the erection of barriers to international trade, and many other measures that can reduce economic growth and employment. These proposals are reported as serious economic statements with little regard for the economic destruction these policies can create.

Why do otherwise sensible people support bad economic policy? It has to be that they have not ever seriously considered the discipline of economics and realized that there is a great difference between economic fiction and economic fact. They do not seem to realize that just believing something does not make it reasonable, possible, or desirable.

As a general aviation pilot, I am struck by the parallels between piloting an aircraft and commonsense economic policy. Aircraft have many dials and gauges, but three are what I call the stay-alive gauges—plus, of course, the fuel gauge. The altitude indicator is important to be sure that you are flying high enough to avoid the ground or anything attached to the ground. The airspeed indicator needs to be attended to since it is important not to be so slow that the aircraft falls out of the sky and not to be so fast that the wings get ripped off. The attitude indicator is essential to making sure that the pitch of the aircraft and the aircraft wings are in a safe configuration.

It does not matter whether the pilot is a Democrat, a Republican, a member of another party, or an independent. The pilot has to pay attention to these gauges or bad things happen.

It is no different when it comes to economic policy. If you violate the basic principles around which economic decisions are made, bad things will happen. No one can repeal the laws of supply and demand, the freedom and efficiency of private property, or the incentive role of profits in creating production. In addition, if the government grows too large and interferes with the economy too much, the airspeed of the economy will be slowed and, at the extremes, it can result in an (excuse the pun) economic crack-up.

Many young students come to our universities with scant understanding of the basic principles of economics, and they frequently emerge four or five years later with little improvement in their condition. With the exception of business majors, most college graduates never take even one course in economics. It is unfortunate that we issue college degrees to people who have never seriously studied this essential discipline, some of whom will, at some later date, attempt to influence state and national economic policy.

With this in mind, I have set out to remedy this situation with a book about what citizens need to know about economics. All one needs to do is become familiar with the following pages in order to have a general understanding of some of the critical economic issues of our times. I hope you will read the following pages with interest and perhaps pass this copy on to one of your friends. This is particularly a good idea if your friend has never had a course in economics. You never know, perhaps you and your friend will actually become excited about this whole idea of sensible economic policy. It's like one of my students told me after class one day, "Professor Rankin, I can't believe it. I actually like this stuff."

It could happen to you.

CHAPTER 1

How Many Isms Do You Understand?

According to Nobel Prize–winning economist Milton Friedman, "there is only one alternative to free markets. Force: some people telling other people what to do."[1] One of the most powerful quotes of our time, this statement sums up what citizens can expect when their nation departs from capitalism en route to some other ism.

The great Austrian economist Ludwig von Mises observed, "There are two methods for the conduct of affairs within the frame of human society—i.e., peaceful cooperation among men. One is bureaucratic management; the other is profit management."[2]

Friedman told us that we can have free markets or force, and von Mises explained that there is the profit system (capitalism), and then there is bureaucracy. With such a clear choice, why would any people choose force and bureaucracy? The reason is that many generally do not fully understand the choices, and because those who would like to use both force and bureaucracy to accomplish their objectives do their best to cloud and confuse the issues.

The collapse of communism dealt a serious blow to those who have extolled the virtues of the socialist state (communist version). The virtues, it happened, never materialized, and the faults have become evident to the entire world. As it turned out, total State control of the economy and the lives of its people have consistently produced both economic and social disaster.

Communism is a system where the State owns and controls the productive resources. Private property is virtually nonexistent, and the State organizes the factors of production according to whichever plan is in vogue at the time. As a result, the initiative of the workers is destroyed and productivity suffers. The story is told of a visiting American economics professor who asked a Soviet worker why his pace of work was so slow. "Well," was the reply, "we pretend to work, and they pretend to pay us."

In 1991, I had the opportunity to see firsthand the economic conditions in Moscow and Saint Petersburg. This was in the fall, just before the USSR ceased to exist later that year. It was plain to see that a so-called modern communist state was no match for US-style capitalism. Consumer goods were scarce, and the lines for basic foodstuffs like milk and bread were everywhere. The Russians were waiting for hours where we would be all hot under the collar if we had to wait for an extra minute or two at the checkout. Citizens of Moscow stood in line for the basics while we had stores full of everything from electric garage door openers to fishhook sharpeners.

During the tour, our Saint Petersburg tour guide, perhaps infected with freedom fever, pointed across the Neva River to a vintage warship moored at the dock with a Soviet flag flying from the mast. "That is the cruiser *Aurora* that fired the blank shot in 1917 to signal the beginning of the October Russian revolution. We refer to this vessel as the most powerful ship in the Soviet navy: one blank shot followed by seventy-four years of destruction."

Another old Soviet joke refers to a Soviet citizen who called in to have an electrician come and make some repairs to his apartment. He was told that the repairman would arrive the next year on April 14. The citizen asked whether it would be in the morning or the afternoon. The bureaucrat wanted to know why it made any difference since the date was the next year. The citizen replied, "I need to know, because the plumber is coming in the afternoon."

We call communism autocratic socialism. With this type of socialism, if you don't like the way things are, the State uses force to ensure that you cooperate anyway. Communism can be brutally destructive to individual freedoms, and the citizen loses most of his or her rights as an individual. The leaders of the old USSR used to claim that it had no unemployment. I joked with my students that the reason there must be no unemployment is that the government would put up a sign that said, "All unemployed Soviet citizens, please report to the Siberian railway station. By the way, bring a warm coat and a sack lunch." Since no one ever showed up, there must be no unemployment.

The point is that a communist state can indeed eliminate unemployment by forcing all citizens to work. They may not like the work, it may not be pleasant, but it will be work. This is not something we would be willing to accept in the United States.

The difference between autocratic socialism (communism) and market socialism is the method of intimidation. Communism uses the gun and the sword (or the Gulag) to force compliance with its plans and policies. Market socialism attempts to gain the benefits of the marketplace but then uses the power of the bureaucracy to gain compliance from its citizens with a host of rules and regulations. In socialistic countries, the government frequently uses the threat of criminal and civil penalties, sometimes with multiple damages, to force compliance. Most regulation in these countries carries heavy penalties for noncompliance. These penalties may include prison time as well.

Socialism cannot survive without the coercive power of government.

The problem with market socialism is that it requires a large government bureaucracy to force compliance with all the rules and regulations. This takes a lot of tax revenue, so taxes necessarily take a high percentage of the national income. In addition, all these laws infringe upon the exercise of freedom by the nation's citizens and produce general discontent with the functioning of government itself. Another unpleasant effect is that all this meddling in the daily affairs of the nation tends to retard economic vitality and growth.

Fascism is another manifestation of the all-powerful central government approach to running a society and an economy. Fascism relies on one-party rule, and other parties simply are not tolerated. Nationalism is a strong theme of this system, but it must fit into the mold created by the central government. Liberal democracy is simply not tolerated at all. The economy of a fascist society is mixed with an attempt to take advantage of the benefits of entrepreneurship, but without letting it run so far as to interfere with the ruling party. Fascism also has within it the seeds of its own destruction as it tramples on the freedoms of its citizens and does not produce the economic benefits of a free market economy.

In his blockbuster book *1984*, George Orwell presented a picture of the heavy hand of government in a centrally controlled society and economy. Written in 1949, the book is interestingly current as we examine communism and also see the expansion of government interference in market economies. As the reader discovers the terms "doublethink," "thought-crimes," and "newspeak," they remind us of the progressive and politically correct pressures that can be exerted on ordinary citizens. The famous line from his book—"BIG BROTHER IS WATCHING YOU"—has relevance today as the power and influence of central government seems to be growing worldwide.[3]

The political correctness of the present day infringes on the First Amendment to the United States Constitution by pressuring citizens with regard to the very words they use. This is too close to the coercive environment Orwell described in *1984*. Attacks on the First Amendment are attacks on freedom. In addition, economies cannot function efficiently with political correctness as the guide.

A society can become so politically correct that it becomes stupid.

If all of this seems unnecessarily critical of government, remember to keep this in perspective. Government and bureaucracy are both necessary and essential, but government should not move into areas best left to the marketplace. For those who provide the essential functions of government, this policy will ensure that these departments are properly financed rather than made to play second fiddle to the tendencies of government to interfere elsewhere. If the government were to stick to business, the police would be amply funded, prisons would be sufficient to hold criminals, highways would be free of potholes, and the judicial system would have the resources to see that justice is administered. However, such has not been the case in recent years in the United States. Government, particularly at the federal level, has wandered far afield, squandering resources on a grand scale and often with very bad results.

The choice for the United States is clear: force or free markets, bureaucracy or profit management. It would be great to hope for utopia, where everyone is wonderfully happy and has all the income they could dream of. Nevertheless, comparing our economy to utopia is senseless. We must compare the real with the real—our economy with other real economies, our economy with Greece or Italy, France or China—then we can discuss real differences.

CHAPTER 2

Just What Is Capitalism Anyway?

Many Americans do not really know what capitalism is. They realize it has something to do with free enterprise and profit but may not really be able to articulate more than that. If capitalism is so great, and if it has produced so many economic benefits for so many, don't we really need to know what it is? If we don't, how are we going to protect it so that it lasts through this century? To begin, let's look at the cornerstones of capitalism.

Private property is the first cornerstone of capitalism. If an individual can own property, then he or she is more free than a person who can't. It is also an issue of efficiency. Private property is simply used more efficiently than public property because it is in the citizen's best interest to see to it. I think we are all aware that our own personal automobile gets better care from us than the company truck.

Societies that emphasize private property seem to always outproduce those that don't, and by a wide margin.

Americans, for the most part, have the opportunity to enter the occupation of their choice and to start their own business if they choose. This is freedom of enterprise, which I will call the opportunity cornerstone. We pursue our own self-interest by going into business; and in doing so, we promote the national interest.

The students in my classes over the years have not been there to promote the national interest; they were there to promote their own self-interest. However, in the process, they have become part of a better-educated workforce that benefits every citizen in the nation. As our citizens make their own decisions about what they will study, what occupations they choose, and what businesses they will go into, the nation benefits. Entrepreneurs stay up late at night planning their next venture, and in doing so, they help provide the fantastic selection of goods and services we take for granted each and every day in the US. This illustrates the concept of the "invisible hand" developed by the great Scottish economist Adam Smith. Smith wrote *The Wealth of Nations* in 1776, which set forth the idea that self-interest promotes the national interest. In his book, Smith made the following observation: "By pursuing his own interests, he frequently promotes that of society more effectually than when he really intends to promote it." He makes it clear that pursuing your own self-interest is a good thing—if it is done legally and ethically.[1]

Competition (another cornerstone) and capitalism go together like milk and cereal. They cannot exist without each other. When consumers have choices, businesses have to work hard to stay competitive, and in the process, they provide the goods and services that we want and at good prices. Wherever you find poor service and high prices, competition has probably been tampered with. This is particularly the case with government-sponsored or protected monopolies.

Wherever competition exists, the customer benefits, the economy is more productive, and our competitiveness with international producers is maintained. The economics textbooks generally define competition as "many buyers and many sellers, operating independently, with freedom of entry to and exit from the market." This is competition, and with it comes economic benefits no other economic system can match.

The price system (the operational cornerstone) is an almost magical process that provides incentives for the production of goods and services and allocates them with incredible speed and efficiency.

However, it seems that we always get really indignant and want the government to step in anytime the price of some good or service goes up significantly over a short period. However, prices transmit information; and if the prices are held artificially low, the information transmitted is incorrect. If the market is allowed to work, then the higher prices will signal that the production of the good or service should be increased. The resulting increase in production can lead to lower prices, and the consumer will have more of the product that has experienced the price increases. This is a win for the consumer—more for less.

Capitalism works when the price system sets the prices of goods and services. As long as competition exists, supply and demand will set the best possible price and provide the optimal amount of the product. In the late 1970s, President Jimmy Carter limited the purchase of gasoline to every other day depending on the last number on a citizen's license plate; this was to deal with gasoline shortages in the US. The Iran-Iraq War had disrupted oil supplies in the '70s and contributed to the shortages. In January of 1981, the newly inaugurated president Ronald Reagan's first executive order was to deregulate the price of oil and natural gas in the US. Many claimed that gasoline might go up to $3.00 a gallon. In fact, some were calling for the issuance of ration tickets to deal with the shortage. However, in a short time, the reverse happened. Gasoline prices started to trend downward. After peaking in 1980 at $1.31 per gallon, gasoline had declined to $0.86 by 1986. The price system proved that the "we are running out of oil" doomsayers were dead wrong. Looking at the oil supply today, it is hard to believe the price control group could have been so wrong.[2]

Profit (the entrepreneurial cornerstone) is another essential element of the capitalistic system of economics. The opportunity to earn a profit provides for the key factor of production, which is the entrepreneur. The entrepreneur (risk-taking businessperson) is the one who organizes the land, labor, and capital necessary for every business to operate. The profit the firm earns is the compensation for all this hard work and risk-taking.

If the profits of the business are quite high and the owners start driving an expensive automobile and building a big new home, then competition is just around the corner. Others will soon say, "Hey, this looks like a great business. Let's get into it." Then as more businesses are formed, not only will the consumer get lower prices, a lot more of the good or service will be made available. More producers in the market will certainly lower prices, and they could move so low that some of the businesses may be forced out. As this process continues, the price for this product will soon settle at a point where the business is earning what economists call a normal profit.

Remember, profits are a method of compensating the entrepreneur for running the business. If competition is healthy, these profits will be reasonable compensation for their efforts and their willingness to risk their resources in a business venture. They provide the essential ingredient to make capitalism function with amazing efficiency.

It is also important to remember that for corporate America, after-tax profits go in two directions. One is dividends, which reward investors who provide capital to the company, and the rest goes back into the business to enable growth and job creation. It is important to remember that this investment capital is provided voluntarily by citizens and other investors and does not require taxes to provide the goods and services the business produces.

A final cornerstone of capitalism is a limited role for government. This is an important part of the Constitution of the United States and was certainly supported by the founders of the nation. In his first inaugural address, Thomas Jefferson referred to the hope for a "wise and frugal government, which shall restrain men from injuring one another, which shall leave them otherwise free to regulate their own pursuits of industry and improvement, and shall not take from the mouth of labor the bread it has earned."[3] A smoothly functioning and efficient government is essential to capitalism. However, government should concentrate on those areas where it does best and leave to the private sector those areas where it performs best.

Those nations and economies that employ capitalism have nearly always enjoyed a much more rapid rate of economic growth and a higher standard of living for its citizens. The greater the extent to which capitalism is employed, the greater have been the economic benefits. The Economic Freedom of the World index created by the Cato Institute measures economic freedom worldwide. The nations at the top of the list (Hong Kong, Singapore, and New Zealand are the top three) have significantly higher per capita incomes than nations with less freedom. It is interesting that the United States currently ranks sixteenth; and as recently as 2000, it was ranked second. The US had been in the top ten for decades. The change in the ranking for the United States has been significant and troubling. It is also important to note that the nations in the top 25% of the index have a per capita gross domestic product approximately seven times that of the nations in the bottom 25%.[4] It seems reasonable to say that freedom with regard to economic choices is significantly related to economic prosperity and that capitalism involves a great deal of economic freedom.

> *In capitalism, citizens benefit themselves by producing something of value. In socialism, they do so by learning how to work the system.*

Talented people prosper either way. However, they will do very different things under socialism in order to get ahead. In addition, the economic results are very different for ordinary citizens. The more of our citizens who are engaged in the production of goods and services, the more we will have and the more affordable it will be.

The growth and size of our central government must be controlled before socialism is so entrenched that we cannot return to the time-honored concept of "doing it yourself." Entire departments of the federal government need to be disbanded or significantly downsized. Programs need to be eliminated and federal taxes need to be cut to restore incentives to work and invest. Make no mistake, for the past eighty years, we have slowly acquired a lot of socialism, and it is past time to reverse the trend. The size and scope of the federal government must be limited in order to preserve both freedom and the free market. In 1992, former president Ronald Reagan remarked, "We have long since discovered that nothing lasts longer than a temporary government program."[5] It is worth remembering that the military draft lasted for nearly thirty years (1940–1973) after the conclusion of World War II.

It is also important to remember that the closer to the people government is, the more efficient it is likely to be. You can catch the mayor on the sidewalk and give him or her your views on city government. It is a lot more difficult to have a real impact on events in Washington. It is unfortunate that we have sent so much of our income to Washington (courtesy of the Sixteenth Amendment) when most of the challenges citizens face each day are a lot closer to home.

CHAPTER 3

We're From the Government,
and We Are Here to Help You

It is not unusual for free market advocates to be accused of being opposed to government. Nothing could be further from the truth. The efficient functioning of government is essential to a strong free market economy, and it is certainly one of the reasons the United States has shown such strong economic growth during its nearly 250-year history.

It is absolutely imperative for the United States to maintain a sound currency, an efficient system of transportation, an honest and efficient judicial system, an effective process of law enforcement, and a strong national defense. Contracts must be honored, merchandise must not be hijacked on the way to the market, the currency must hold its value, and the transportation system of the country must be safe and reliable. These are the conditions necessary for sound and rapid economic development—along with the existence of a free market, of course.

All these conditions have been present in the American situation. It would be nice to give ourselves credit for being smart, having good natural resources, being educated, and all that. However, other societies have had these advantages, and yet they have not produced the economic miracle of the United States. But for the most part, particularly prior to the 1930s, the American government has confined itself to providing a healthy environment for economic development and refrained from entering into the marketplace itself. The result has been the development of the most powerful economy in the history of mankind.

> *Government has an absolutely essential role to play in a free market economy.*

The better it plays its role, the faster the rate of economic development will be, and the better the economic lives of its citizens. But since the explosion in the growth of government during the Great Depression (1929–1939), more and more economic decisions are being interfered with by government bureaucracy. It is this interference with the economic market that is producing many of the national problems we witness today. This meddling is producing poverty, expanding government payrolls, creating pressure for higher taxes, expanding the national debt, and generating a growing dissatisfaction in the general population with the effectiveness of government, particularly at the federal level.

The title of this chapter is taken from a quip that originated during the Great Depression, as the role of government expanded. It was a tongue-in-cheek poking of fun at the army of newly created bureaucrats that suddenly appeared bearing gifts, or so they said. It should remind us that government does not hatch these benefits out of thin air. It either borrows the dollars or it takes them from an individual who earned them in the marketplace. Government does not create jobs; it simply reallocates them from the private marketplace to the government. For every employee hired by the government, there will be at least one (and sometimes more than one) fewer employees hired by business and industry. This is not to say that government—by providing the basics of transportation, the judicial system, and so forth—does not create an environment where more jobs can be created. It does. However, when government gets into the business of hiring simply to reallocate income from one person to the other, that is a different situation. In this instance, the jobs gained in government are generally lost in the private sector. The situation can actually be worse than it appears. If a government employee is engaged in a program that actually does damage to the economy, and the private-sector employee would have most certainly produced something valuable, the loss is obvious. The economy loses the production of the private employee and substitutes the services of the public employee, who may actually damage the economy (by creating bucketloads of rules and regulations, for example). It is interesting to note that Thomas Jefferson (in the Declaration of Independence in 1776) complained that King George III "has erected a multitude of new offices and sent hither swarms of officers to harass our people, and eat out their substance."[1] Obviously, Jefferson was as concerned then, as many are now, about the runaway meddling of central governments.

There are so many dedicated employees of the federal, state, and local governments who are essential to the functioning of the free market. Economic growth would be either impossible or seriously damaged without them. Police officers, mayors, firefighters, highway department employees, judges, and, without question, the valuable members of our armed forces—all are indispensable to a market economy. Without national defense, the barbarians would break down the gates, and we would lose everything.

However, this does not mitigate the fact that many government employees spend their time with duties that either do little to promote the national good or actually damage the economy of the nation. They could be in the private sector producing clothing, food, automobiles, houses, computers, travel services, transportation services, and a host of other economic goods and services. Instead, they toil away with the best of intentions, and at great expense to the taxpayer, when they could be productive in the private sector. All because government has gotten into the business of interfering with the economic marketplace, which would be better off without it.

Milton Friedman, in *Free to Choose*, addresses the growth of government programs that have been developed to deal with problems created by other government programs by saying this:

The situation would be ludicrous if it were not so serious. While many of these effects cancel out, their costs do not. Each program takes money from our pockets that we could use to buy goods and services to meet our separate needs. Each of them uses able, skilled people who could be engaged in productive activities. Each one grinds out rules, regulations, red tape, forms to fill in that bedevil us all.[2]

The many thousands of employees engaged in these activities could be in the private marketplace producing goods and services that would raise everyone's standard of living. Surely, we would all be better off if the government put more resources into its basic essential services and quit meddling in the economy, where it does lot of damage and wastes our precious tax revenue.

We have all heard the phrase Money Is Power. There is a lot of truth to this statement, and it certainly applies to government. The fifty state governments certainly do have power, but it is small by comparison to Washington. If you send a thousand bureaucrats to Washington and tell them to regulate something, that is what they will do. If this happens on a large scale, the economy will begin to be slowly strangled by thousands of regulations created by well-meaning people doing their jobs each day. Many Americans have had the experience of waiting and waiting for some government agency to tell them if they can proceed with a certain activity that would make common sense to most people. This process can slow innovation and economic activity and actually creates a loss of freedom to run our own lives. Moreover, this does not count the cost of the government activity, where the money will come from, or the lost production if these individuals were working in the private sector and producing something of value.

It is critical to look at every government policy to discover its impact on liberty. Our passion for liberty is what makes the United States different from all the other nations of the world. We have historically valued liberty, and this ingredient permeates the Constitution and the Bill of Rights. Nations who have made a habit of sacrificing liberty for security are a dime a dozen. Nations who have a habit of protecting and promoting liberty are as scarce as a hen's teeth.

We all know that human wants are insatiable and unlimited. We need to remember that the wants of government fall into the same category. Government—particularly a central government—seems to always want more resources and to develop all kinds of reasons as to why this is a good idea. It is one thing if it gets these resources as a result of the growth of the economy. It is another thing if the share of the economy in citizens' hands begins to shrink. This involves a loss of freedom.

The bottom line is that there is a strong tendency for government to get involved in areas that are best left to the marketplace. In addition, the level of funding for a federal agency may or may not be appropriate for the goal of the activity. A government agency with too many employees is a prescription for regulatory overload. That this situation can exist at the same time that an essential agency is starved for employees is just the nature of government. In the private sector, the pressures of the marketplace take care of this issue. The only way for citizens to deal with this is to limit the size of the central government. When new programs always seem to involve new money, then the situation is basically hopeless. There will never be any pressure for cost-effective operations that would require the reallocation of resources.

State and local governments have a much greater incentive for efficiency because their resources are limited. Nearly all the states have a balanced budget requirement so that they cannot borrow just to meet the day-to-day budget. With the federal government, it is a different situation. Due to the immense borrowing capacity of Washington, it is easy to keep spending on whatever and just sell some more bonds. This means that the central government is not going to be sensible about what it spends money on. The political pain for our elected representatives for cutting programs is just too high. The day of reckoning will only come when the interest rate on government debt gets so high that it crowds out other government spending to the extent that something has to be done. This day is not tomorrow, but if we continue in our current direction, it is coming.

Of course, individual state and local governments can also get carried away with too much taxation and regulation. However, there is a sort of self-regulatory force at work that can bring some common sense back to the table. Particularly within the US, people do have mobility. They can pack up, move to a state that is more accommodative, and leave a state that has become too expensive or too difficult to live in. Many times, those who are moving are not the type of citizens that you would like to lose. In particular, retirees (who are looking at a new phase of life) are more open to a move. In doing so, they tend to look at the states that make the lists of good places to live. There is no question that states that have a small or no income tax, or do not tax retiree income, are attractive magnets.

In the process, the high-tax states can suffer population losses, and the lower-tax states can benefit. These population movements can, in some cases, bring some common sense back to the states that are suffering the losses. There is always a chance that this reality dose can bring about a change in state policy as a matter of survival.

Remember, government benefits come at a cost. The "free lunch" has not arrived just because it comes from government. At this point in our financial history, if you want the federal government to spend more money on a particular project without reallocating spending, you are really supporting a higher level of taxation or a higher level of the national debt, neither of which is desirable.

We want government to do the things it does best. My best example is the traffic light. It provides for the safe and orderly flow of traffic but does not tell me which way to turn or prevent me from going straight ahead. In fact, most of us appreciate this particular role of government. It makes sense, it improves safety, and it doesn't tax us when we proceed through the intersection. Government is an essential ingredient when it comes to economic growth and an orderly and safe society. And, of course, we all appreciate the valuable personnel of law enforcement when we have a traffic accident or need help. We do appreciate those blue lights that signal help is coming. The police are part of the essential public services that need to be properly funded.

When it comes to government, all we citizens ask for is a little common sense. Freedom for our nation will be stronger as a result.

CHAPTER 4

The Federal Explosion: What Happened?

Nearly 250 years ago, the American experiment in liberty was launched with all the gusto of a moon shot and with just as much determination. Patrick Henry's "Give me liberty, or give me death" still echoes across the land, and America still has many of the characteristics of greatness and liberty pulsing through her veins.[1]

Something, however, seems amiss, and citizens almost need to return to dusty books to rediscover just what Patrick Henry meant by "liberty." It seems that something has indeed happened down the path of freedom as government has grown and its interference with the lives of its citizens has expanded.

It's almost like awakening from a long sleep to find that things have changed a little more than you first thought. That somehow, there has been a fundamental change in the basic principles of democracy and you're not really sure how it all happened. Is it true that the balance of power has shifted in favor of a central government and away from individual liberty? And if so, just how did it happen under our watchful eye?

Although running the risk of being too simplistic, I would like to suggest that the transfer of power from the individual to the federal bureau, department, and agency was accomplished largely through none other than the US tax code, via the federal income tax.

The levy of an income tax required the passage of the Sixteenth Amendment to the US Constitution.

Passed in 1913, the amendment reads, "The Congress shall have the power to levy and collect taxes on incomes, from whatever source derived, without apportionment among the several states, and without regard to any census or enumeration." It is important to note that the amendment did not provide for any limitation as to how much of anyone's income could be collected as taxes. In addition, there is no guideline as to the nature of the tax or any provision for sharing the proceeds of the tax with the states or local government.[2]

How innocent did the first income tax appear in 1913, beginning at 1% on the first $20,000 (adjusted for inflation, that's equivalent to $508,259 today) and reaching a maximum of 7% on all income over $500,000 (over $12,706,465 today). So innocent, in fact, that Americans virtually ignored opposition and moved cheerfully along, hauling this "Trojan horse" into the pocketbooks of America. My, how small beginnings multiply! Surely, most supporters of the income tax never envisioned that the technique would ultimately be used to redistribute a massive share of the national income to Washington, DC.[3]

Using the financial requirements of World War I, supporters of the income tax raised the top marginal rate to an incredible 77%. The war ended, but the rates never returned to their original levels. Then along came the Great Depression as our Federal Reserve System watched and allowed our banking system to crumble. It ushered in the Great Depression, followed by an explosion of federal government spending to try to stimulate the economy. It was actually World War II that energized the economy and put Americans to war and to work and again provided new support for high marginal tax rates on income. Victory seemed to have little effect on the tax rates, and the dollars kept rolling to Washington. In fact, it was President Kennedy in 1963 who led the charge to cut personal and corporate income tax rates and provide the first supply-side version tax cut in modern US history. He recognized that high tax rates were becoming an impediment to economic growth in the US. The Revenue Act of 1964 was signed into law by President Lyndon Johnson on February 26, 1964. The law reduced the top personal income rate from 91% to 70% and the top corporate rate from 52% to 47%. Although Kennedy was killed in Dallas in the fall of 1963, much of the credit belongs to him for leading this effort.[4]

> *President Kennedy was actually a supply-sider before it was cool.*

It is certainly true that during periods of war, large portions of personal and business income must be allocated to national defense. However, with the lack of such an event, it is certainly not reasonable for government to continue to take a large part of a person's or a corporation's income. The negative impact upon economic decisions—such as the desire to work, save, and invest—can be substantial. In addition, the basic concept of the freedom to spend one's own income is an essential element of liberty, and this is violated by high income tax rates.

Interestingly enough, it was inflation that provided the next boost for the federal treasury as taxpayers began to be rapidly propelled into higher and higher tax brackets. In addition, the movement of more women to work outside the home boosted family taxable income, and provided an added spurt to federal tax revenues, as Americans suddenly discovered that "them is us" in referring to high tax bracket Americans. The run on the American pocketbook accelerated, and with the Washington financial express grew government buildings, bureaucrats, grants, federal aid, procedures, regulations, and a virtual explosion of the federal presence. In fact, the flow of dollars to Washington has been so powerful that it almost appears some agencies have really, at times, been pressed to find ways to deploy the funds.

By the late '70s, the US economy had plowed itself into slow economic growth, and yet average Americans continued to be propelled into higher and higher tax brackets due to inflation. In the fall of 1980, the inflation rate was running at 1½% per month, the unemployment rate was 7.4%, and in January of 1981, the prime rate of interest reached an all-time high of 21½%. US economic problems were certainly instrumental in the defeat of President Carter by Ronald Reagan in 1980.[5]

To boost the economy, the new Reagan administration promoted the Economic Recovery Act of 1981. The 25% across-the-board personal income tax cuts included in the Act put dollars back into private hands. In addition, for the first time, federal income tax brackets were indexed to inflation. No longer would Americans pay higher taxes due just to inflation.[6] By the summer of 1982, the stock market started moving up, and the economy was soon in a healthy economic recovery with much lower interest rates and inflation. The 1981–82 recession was brutal, but a combination of fiscal and monetary policy, including some deficit spending, put the country back on the path of economic growth. During 1983 and 1984, the economy began a strong expansion and was a primary reason for the landslide reelection of Reagan in the fall of 1984.

A quote from former president Ronald Reagan seems to sum up the attitude of too many of our government leaders, particularly at the national level. In 1986, at a White House Conference on Small Business, he remarked, "Back then [before his administration], government's view of the economy could be summed up in a few short phrases. If it moves, tax it. If it keeps moving, regulate it. And if it stops moving, subsidize it."[7] His position was that the tax cuts of 1981 and 1986 had reversed this policy.

Even with these federal tax rate reductions, federal revenues only declined in 1983 and then continued to grow until 2001. Actually, the period spanning 1983 through 2001 was a time when federal revenue grew at a faster rate than federal spending, resulting in a federal budget surplus in 1998 for the first time in thirty years.[8] I believe that this is strong evidence that tax reductions that improve the rate of national economic growth can also result in strong federal revenue growth.

President Reagan's economic plan was frequently referred to by its critics as "trickle-down economics." It was a term that stuck and continues to be used today. However, the plan had little to do with economic benefits trickling down to the consumer. The personal tax cuts went directly into the after-tax paychecks of millions of American workers as they began to take effect. By contrast, the spending of money by Washington is much more reflective of the term. It can be summed up much more appropriately in the following way:

Send your money to Washington, and maybe some of it will trickle down to your house.

Trickle-down economics is much more descriptive of the large government-spending package enacted in 2009 by the Obama administration. There is no question that spending on various government projects can have a positive impact on most any economy; but it is not instant, and it does take time for the benefits to trickle down to ordinary citizens.

Americans must realize that strong economic growth depends on moderate personal and business income tax rates. An essential ingredient for America is a free economy, and a free economy is hampered when the federal government controls a large share of the national income. The fact is that any government that has high progressive income tax rates, and the citizens actually pay what they owe, will most certainly be able to appropriate a large portion of national income for its own purposes.

Examine the case. Hasn't the highly progressive income tax allowed the federal government to grow to its size today? Hasn't this tax system allowed the capture of a large share of the national income by Washington? In 1930, federal revenue as a percent of gross domestic product (total US production) was 4.4%. Today it is approximately 18%. And remember, this is only federal revenue and does not count state, county, and city revenues.[9] The federal personal income tax started out in 1913 with a 7% top rate, and today (2018), the top rate personal rate is 37.0%. This top rate does not include the state rate if you live in a state with a personal income tax.

The first step in holding the line on Washington's share of the national income is to protect indexing for our children, our grandchildren, and us. It's worth trillions of dollars in tax savings for Americans and future Americans. The second step is a reduction in the progressive tax rates. As you now know, President Kennedy cut the top personal rate to 70%, and President Reagan cut it again to 50% and then to 28%. It is interesting to note that both presidents— one a Republican and one a Democrat—realized that too much federal government is bad economic policy. The top marginal rate was increased during the George H. W. Bush administration to 31%, and then to 39.6% by the Clinton administration. It was reduced back to 35% during the George W. Bush administration and then increased back to 39.6% during the Obama administration. The Trump administration's Tax Cuts and Jobs Act of 2017 cut the top bracket to 37%. A return to the top rate of 28% of the Reagan years would be a wise goal for the future.

It is very interesting that the federal revenue percentage of gross domestic product has ranged between 15% and 19% over the past seventy years regardless of whether the tax rates were being cut or increased. This tends to indicate that you can only squeeze so much out of an economy with an income tax due to tax avoidance, tax evasion, and other decisions with regard to the creation of taxable income.[10]

Americans need a federal government that is focused on federal responsibilities and economic growth, not one that tries to solve every problem imaginable.

Today's mind-set seems to be that Washington can make anything better if it just spends enough money. However, a free economy cannot function efficiently in an atmosphere of unbridled government spending. The very future of our free enterprise system depends upon our recognition of the simple fact that the freedom to spend one's own paycheck is one of America's most essential principles.

CHAPTER 5

Incentives Matter, Don't They?

I have often stated in speeches and in class that if you want more of something, then subsidize it; and if you want less of something, then tax it. If this is indeed the case, then it should come as no surprise that as we tax and regulate work more, we get less of it; and as we subsidize nonwork, we get more of it. Incentives matter! If we have incentives to improve our education and training, work hard, and move to get that good job, then that is the type of things we will do. If we have incentives to meet the guidelines for certain government benefit programs, then we might do that.

In response to the devastation of the Great Depression, President Roosevelt and his planners devised a variety of programs to deal with the massive unemployment and economic collapse of that time. Although we must give Mr. Roosevelt credit for trying to restore the economic fortunes of the United States, we must remember that it was the failure of the Federal Reserve System to protect the banking system that caused the disaster in the first place. The Federal Reserve stood by while one-third of the banks in the US failed and the money supply declined by the same proportion. The result of all this was predictable: an economic depression, and a long one at that. If the Federal Reserve System had done its job properly, the Great Depression would never have happened, and the explosive growth of the federal government during the '30s would not have occurred.

Socialism in the United States received a tremendous boost due to the Depression. President Roosevelt adopted the economic philosophy of British economist John Maynard Keynes, who in 1936 wrote the *General Theory of Employment, Interest, and Money*, in which he advocated government spending as the primary method of dealing with economic depression.[1] There is not much controversy that the spending of government money can create economic activity. We have a Greek theater on campus that was completed in 1937 under the direction of the Works Projects Administration. This was an effort to put young men to work and deal with the tremendous level of unemployment that existed at the time. The pay was low, but it was cash, and it helped individuals and families hold things together. One of the faculty members I knew had worked on this project as a young man, grateful to have a way to make some money.

The result was an explosion of government spending during the Depression, followed by the necessary but dramatic World War II spending, which has helped create a federal government that now spends an amount equal to 18%–20% of the total production of the nation. By the way, it was economist Milton Friedman who should get most of the credit for documenting the real cause of the Depression. He pointed out in *Free to Choose* that it was not the stock market crash or a failure of capitalism that caused the Depression. It was a failure of government.[2]

Therefore, the accelerated growth of the federal government in the 1930s was not the result of some basic need on behalf of the American economy for more government. It came as a result of a financial disaster created in large measure by the federal government itself.

Wouldn't you just know it? Government helped produce a disaster and then took credit for saving us from it. It only makes sense if you are viewing the situation from just north of the Potomac River.

I have told my students over the years that you should never let your banks fail. This was the key to the survival of the US financial system during the financial crisis of 2008–09. Action by the federal authorities was much different from that during the 1930s, and a real disaster was averted. The 2008–09 recession is now referred to as the Great Recession. I refer to it as the 2008–09 financial recession as it was nearly a financial disaster, and we had a number of important financial and investment firms on the brink of collapse. Although this recession was more dangerous than the 1981–82 recession, I do not think it was as bad. Having lived through both, it is an easy call for me.

It is important to understand that programs designed to deal with emergency issues may be very inappropriate for the normal situation. However, governments tend to continue to do whatever it is doing even when the emergency need has ceased to be. This can produce unintended consequences.

At an appearance at our university a number of years ago, economist Walter Williams related an interesting example of the difference between intention and effect, which I have never forgotten. It went like this:

> When you look at policy, you must always pay attention to policy effects—the effects of policy, not the intentions. I could walk out of this building on my way back to Washington, DC, and walk across the highway and a truck could run over me. The truck driver could get out of the truck and say, "Williams, I did not intend to run over you." Well, I am as run over as if he intended.

> When you carry me off to the coroner to discover the cause of death, you don't need to tell the coroner anything about the intentions of the truck driver. The wheels rolling over my body are independent of the intentions of the truck driver. So what you care about are the effects of policy, not the intentions.[3]

It is so important for our elected representatives, whether at the state or national level, to realize that when you establish incentives for a certain behavior, you tend to get that behavior regardless of their intentions. If unemployment insurance runs at full benefits for a certain period, there is a tendency for some to remain unemployed for that period. A phaseout of unemployment benefits would have the benefit of providing temporary help but gradually restoring the incentive to find some type of employment earlier. It is to our advantage to limit our unemployment time as much as possible because our job skills can get out-of-date and rusty.

Poverty benefits can often provide incentives to do what is necessary to meet the guidelines for receiving assistance. When this happens, the incentive to work can be diluted, and the incentive for nonwork is increased. In addition, when individuals do not work, they miss out on the opportunity to participate in the benefits that work provides for promotions and advancement, which generally leads to higher incomes. This situation contributes to a higher level of income inequality in a society that has a significant welfare component. Working citizens improve their lives as the nonworking become trapped in a permanent low-income situation.

> *Anything beyond temporary or transitional assistance*
> *creates a dependency issue.*

This is common sense turned upside down. As one welfare recipient said to a working friend, "I don't see why you go to work. I just go to the mailbox." Today it is not the mailbox, but too many of our government assistance programs have incentives for nonwork. Assistance programs need to be reviewed, and incentives for permanence need to be phased out. The reform of the American welfare system is essential to providing incentives for citizens to move up and ahead, which is essential for expanded economic growth and development. It would also be a healthy step toward reducing income inequality among Americans. Economist Henry Hazlitt put this whole issue in perspective with the following statement:

> The real problem of poverty is not a problem of
> "distribution" but of production. The poor are poor not
> because something is being withheld from them but

because, for whatever reason, they are not producing enough.[4]

In my opinion, we have the wrong incentives for dealing with poverty in the US and across most of the world. In the US system, the less productive lower-income individuals are, the more they are rewarded. This produces an incentive for lower or no production. The incentives need to be targeted toward rewarding preparation for production and for production itself. Otherwise, the gap between the nonproductive and the productive can do no less than get larger and larger.

You can also see how incentives matter by observing our individual states. States (and sometimes local governments too) can get carried away with taxation and regulation in the search for what they might perceive as the ideal society. However, some of these governments are discovering that its citizens can relocate to more citizen-friendly states and communities. Many businesses are geographically mobile and can phase out operations in tax and regulatory unfriendly areas and expand operations in friendly areas or just move completely. It seems clear to me that the high-regulatory, high-tax states are going to struggle in the future in comparison to the low-tax, low-regulatory states. I am not sure why the prosperity of some of these high-tax states seems to accompany a decline in common sense, but it seems to do so with regularity.

Some US states seem to have an economic death wish.

Incentives matter, and the more powerful the incentive, the more it matters. In developing policy, we must be sure that the incentives that are in place promote the activities that are in the best interests of society. It is critical to our national economic future that we eliminate the incentives that promote activity that is destructive to both economic freedom and economic growth.

CHAPTER 6

The Youth Unemployment Maximization Act

Growing up in a small town in the '50s was a low-stress experience where a bicycle and a fishing pole were all that was needed for a great summer. There was no organized entertainment, so we made our own up and down the country lanes of Junction City, Arkansas. It was a time of individual decision-making, and about the only experience with government any of us had was with the US Post Office and our school.

Finding a job was also pretty easy. You could create your own by mowing yards or signing on to do simple tasks for a business or individual in the community. It didn't take much in the way of earnings to provide a little spending money for a Saturday afternoon movie, some BBs for the Red Ryder, or a refreshing five-cent Coke.

One of my most memorable jobs was working for a local man as an assistant for his lawn mower and small-engine repair service. I don't recall a rate per hour, but my boss would share some of the revenues of the business each week, which was okay by me. In the process, I learned to fix about any small engine in town—a skill that is still useful to me today. It was a great deal. I learned how to work and how to say "yes, sir" and do what I was told. I gained a skill and picked up a little pocket change along the way. Nobody talked about the minimum wage in those days, thought much about it, or for that matter, paid much attention to it. Government wasn't big enough to do a whole lot of meddling in people's affairs, and most liked it that way.

I also remember mowing lawns during the summer for a variety of community residents. I just had to invest in a small hand-push mower and a gas can, and I was in business. Since all my living expenses were covered, I could provide a competitive rate, and business was good.

Young people of that day had to find something productive to do or there was no money at all. Parents didn't hand out much, and most young people were expected to do something on their own if they wanted spending money. In the process, a lot of teenagers worked pretty hard, many on the farm. I remember that football practice had to work around the milking schedule or some of the star players just wouldn't be there. The point of all this is that the government didn't spend a lot of time making it difficult for teenagers to work in those days. Most teens that really wanted to work were able to talk someone into hiring them or were able to develop a business of some sort.

> *During the developing years of this country, when agriculture was king, virtually every youngster worked. They milked the cows, slopped the hogs, cut the firewood, washed the clothes, helped cook dinner, and worked at a host of other activities.*

There was no choice, and much of the work was hard. The result was generation after generation of Americans who knew how to work. They learned the skills and discipline that helped them with life in general. There was no minimum wage, no forty-hour workweek, no overtime pay, no nothing—just an opportunity to work. But the work helped build a great nation and a great people who knew how to work, how to be responsible, and what it took to get ahead. One of these groups has been called the Greatest Generation.

Years ago, in one of my classes, a retired gentleman described how he landed a job during the Great Depression. He went to a local banker and offered to work for him for two months without pay. The deal was if the banker liked his work, he would hire him on permanently. The young man went to work and later became a successful banker at the same bank, grateful for the opportunity to get started in work. Today, more and more teens are entering their adult years without ever having had a job. They are not learning how to work, and they are not gaining the experience they need to move on to the next level. Many of those graduating from college are looking for their "first" job.

When you think about it, why should government forbid a contract between one individual who has a job to offer and another who would like to work? It would seem that our constitution would guarantee such a right. However, the minimum wage law does not. If a kid is willing to work for $6.50 per hour but the potential employer is covered by the minimum wage law, too bad. The kid won't work, and the service he would have performed is lost to the economy. In addition, without the job, the youngster might end up in trouble or find something illegal to do—which would, of course, not be in the public interest. By the way, there is no minimum wage for illegal activity and no government benefits, unless they end up in jail with free room and board.

Minimum wage laws only damage the economy and freedom when the minimum is above the market wage for the type of employment covered. If you are worth $10 per hour in the marketplace and the minimum wage is $7.25, then no problem. You are not affected. But if you are worth $7 and the minimum wage is $10, you do have a problem. If you don't become more valuable to potential employers real quick, you will stay unemployed. In recent years, we have seen workers demonstrate for a $15 minimum wage. Some would be doing so not realizing that if they are not worth $15 per hour, they will soon be replaced by more productive employees or by technology. There seems to be a lack of understanding that when prices and wages change, other things change as well.

I have long believed that the minimum wage laws generate unemployment among teenagers in particular because they are young and may have few (if any) job skills.

The only way they are going to be hired is if they can demonstrate good potential. In other words, if you are going to pay a $15 per hour minimum wage, you want the most talented individuals you can find. But what about the less talented? Since you can't offer them less than the minimum to account for their lack of skill, they remain unemployed. Economist Thomas Sowell summed it up in the following way in his 2018 book *Discrimination and Disparities*:

> Similarly, people who discuss raising the government-mandated minimum wage rate talk as if this would automatically mean having the lowest-paid workers' income rise from $10 an hour to $15 per hour, for example. In reality, for millions of inexperienced and unskilled young workers, it can mean that the wages they receive in fact fall from $10 an hour to zero, when they are unable to find jobs.[1]

In addition, it makes little sense to have a minimum wage set by the federal government that applies to the entire nation. A minimum wage of a certain level may have little effect in a high-wage area like Boston, but it could be a significant impediment to employment in a small town in another part of the nation where wage and income levels, and the cost of living, may be only half as much as those in the big city. If the minimum wage were a real minimum wage, it would be the rate per hour that would allow the least qualified worker in the labor pool to find a job.

It is another example of the one-size-fits-all mentality of a centralized government in Washington. A sensible approach to this problem would be for the federal government to get out of the minimum wage business entirely. This way, the high-wage states could set higher levels, and the lower-wage states could set their rates at a level that is more appropriate for them or eliminate the minimum wage entirely. This way, decisions would more likely reflect the economic realities of that particular region of the country. This would also mean that if one state or city wanted to limit opportunities for the unskilled, at least the limitation would not apply to the whole nation.

In addition, why not exempt teens from the minimum wage entirely? Let them work for $7 per hour cleaning up the parking lot. Give them a chance to prove their worth to their employer. The ones who work efficiently will soon get an increase in pay. In any event, the $7 per hour is more than they will be earning hanging around the parking lot instead of cleaning it up. Young people need to learn to work. In the old days, they learned this on the farm. Parents today that have farms or businesses give their children quick lessons in capitalism by putting them to work early and often. Sometimes they get paid, sometimes they don't—but they learn how to work, which is the most valuable benefit.

We obviously have a problem providing job opportunities for the young and unskilled. Let's try something different. Let the marketplace work the way it has for all of man's economic history. Move the minimum wage issue to the states and let them have the flexibility to do what is best for their citizens. If some want to exempt teens or have a lower rate, then let the states do it. Young people will be better off as a result.

CHAPTER 7

Dead-End Jobs: Fact or Fiction?

It seems as though, almost daily, we see an article or TV commentary on the sad situation of "dead-end" jobs in America. The author usually describes America as becoming a nation of hamburger flippers where all the manufacturing jobs are disappearing and are being replaced by low-paying service jobs. This type of economically obsolete talk is shocking to those who understand the statistics that indicate approximately 80% of all jobs in the country today are nonmanufacturing jobs and that this is, in fact, the wave of both the present and the future. Manufacturing production is not decreasing in the US, but employment is due to the tremendous increase in the productivity of our manufacturing sector. At the same time, service jobs are expanding rapidly, and many of these jobs are highly skilled with tremendous opportunities for the future.[1] However, it is important to remember that most workers have had to pay their dues and work their way up the ladder to the higher-paying positions.

Work experience has proven to be particularly valuable in upward job mobility. The term "dead-end job" is a much misapplied term that is frequently used to describe an entry-level job, many of which are in the service area. It must be remembered that most "entry-level" jobs are low-wage simply because the employee normally comes to the job with little or no experience. As experience is gained, the employee moves up in the existing business or gains the job experience necessary to move to another employer at a higher-than-entry-level position. Many employers look for entry-level job experience as a sign of a willingness to work and be consistent in job performance. There is nothing wrong with a low-skill job. In fact, hundreds of thousands of teenagers would just love to have one; but they can't find employment anywhere. We must be careful not to continue to erect barriers to the employment of young and unskilled workers. When the government passes rules and regulations that raise the cost of hiring workers, opportunities for the less skilled and the young are reduced the most.

The primary advantage a low-skilled or young worker offers is a lower cost of employment. If this cost is raised through minimum wage increases, mandatory health care, or other costly regulations and rules, the cost of employment increases and can become so high that low-skilled workers are either not hired at all or only in very small numbers. Those workers who are hired will tend to come from the greater-ability and higher-skilled groups. The low-skilled may be simply priced out of the market and may become permanently unemployed because they never gain the entry-level experience necessary to advance to the more skilled jobs.

Many young Americans will not get those first jobs.

High youth employment rates, particularly among minorities, are a worrisome problem because job experience can significantly expand future employment opportunities. If low-skill entry-level job opportunities are destroyed, many young and unskilled Americans will not be able to get those first jobs that propel them to more attractive opportunities in the job market.[2]

We need to preserve entry-level jobs so that tomorrow's generation can have the opportunity to gain job experience. In order to work one's way up the ladder, one must first get a foot on the first rung. If government cuts off the lower rungs, the aspiring worker may be left standing on the ground floor.

An old story is told of a young man who approached an experienced craftsman with a request to serve as an apprentice. The boy asked how much the craftsman would pay for his labor. The craftsman laughed and said, "Pay you! Young man, you must pay me if you plan to apprentice here and learn this valuable craft." The point is that a young worker may receive a lot more value from the work than he or she is paid in wages. That is, after all, an important reason young people seek these entry-level jobs in the first place. They know that job experience is valuable to their future. A survey of teenagers I conducted a number of years ago in Southwest Arkansas indicated that only a third of teenagers considered their wage to be the most important reason for working. This is probably because most teens live at home and enjoy complimentary room and board. It is certainly not necessary for them to earn an income high enough to support a family in order for them to benefit from their work. The comparison of the minimum wage to the fuzzy concept of a "living wage" is ridiculous. We should not price young people out of the labor market in search of labor force utopia.

I recall visiting with one of my students working at a local retail store. Since he was a business major, I commented that his job was certainly good experience for the future. "Exactly what I think," he replied. "That's why I am working here." This young man clearly recognized that it wasn't the wage that he was receiving that was the big issue—it was the experience. This is a primary reason that internships are so attractive to college students.

I recall interviewing an area businessman who made the following statement: "I pay a young person the minimum wage per hour to work for me, and they get $20 per hour worth of experience." This statement indicates that it is not the wages or benefits that are most important for entry-level jobs. It is the experience. We need to preserve and even promote entry-level jobs, not criticize them as "dead-end." Our economic future depends on today's young people learning to work and getting their feet on the first rung of the economic ladder.

It is certainly desirable to see every American earning a good wage with full job benefits. However, worker productivity must provide for these wages and benefits. They are not free but are provided by the employer, who depends on the company customers who provide the revenue. If we increase the job costs above the productivity of the worker, that worker will soon be unemployed. To force those costs on employers for low-productivity, entry-level jobs will destroy many of these job opportunities. We need to let the marketplace decide on these matters, not the government. The government often searches for pie-in-the-sky solutions, but the job market must deal with realities.

Just what is a dead-end job anyway?

Is it a fourteen-year-old loading hay on the family farm? Is it an eighteen-year-old working her way through college at a fast-food restaurant? Could it be a nineteen-year-old working at a local retail store? All these jobs are entry-level, and certainly, the pay may not be high. In fact, the hay loader may simply get a good meal out of the effort.

The key point is that all these jobs offer experience for the future, an opportunity to learn the discipline and sweat of work. The workers benefit by gaining job experience with which to impress a future employer; and yes, certainly, they earn some monetary compensation to buy books or put gas in the tank. Who benefits if these jobs disappear? Regulations could forbid a fourteen-year-old from doing farm work; the minimum wage could be raised to $20 per hour, which might eliminate the fast-food job, and mandatory health insurance (paid by the employer) could eliminate the retail store job. But this would not help the economy and certainly not these three young people. If they can continue to gain experience, then they will soon qualify for jobs that command higher wages and full benefits. If these were really dead-end jobs, these three young people would still be in the same position five years from now. But they won't; they will have moved on up the ladder to a better economic future. For them, these jobs were entry-level jobs, not dead-end jobs. There are millions of entry-level jobs in America, and they offer an opportunity for a better future to all who hold them.

Working for a living is a cornerstone of American culture and economy.

To preserve the work ethic, it is essential that we do not condemn or belittle those who are trying to build a better life for themselves and, in so doing, build a better future for our nation.

America's great theologian and evangelist Billy Graham had this to say about the value of labor:

> Labor Day should remind us also of the dignity and importance of our work in God's eyes. God gave us the ability to work, and no matter what our job is, we should see it as a God-given responsibility that He wants us to do faithfully and well. Jesus worked most of His life as a carpenter, and I'm sure His doors always fit and His tables didn't wobble.[3]

Adults today can always remember their first job, whether it was delivering papers, mowing lawns, helping in the family business, babysitting, feeding the cows, or doing chores for the neighbors. These experiences create in the minds of young people an understanding that goods and services do not fall out of the sky. They are created through labor. This helps create citizens who know instinctively that they must labor for a better life and cannot stand by and wait for someone to hand them a living.

In fact, one of the best gifts we can give to our children and grandchildren is to impress upon them the importance and value of work. The future of our nation depends on a citizenry that puts the value of work at the forefront of our personal and national priorities.

CHAPTER 8

Taxation without Common Sense
(We have the representation,
but the common sense is missing)

As mentioned in chapter 4, we Americans, in our less than infinite wisdom, passed the Sixteenth Amendment to the Constitution in 1913 in order to create an income tax in the United States. The Supreme Court had previously declared an income tax unconstitutional. The states then took four years to amend the Constitution to allow for the income tax, but they did not include any limits on its amount. The final result of all this was rates reaching 91% during World War II. In addition, the Sixteenth Amendment did not provide for sharing income tax revenue with the states.

We call our federal income tax system a progressive tax. This means, in my opinion, that it gets progressively worse as your income increases. At the present time (2018), we have brackets of 10%, 12%, 22%, 24%, 32%, 35%, and 37% on income subject to federal income taxes. Most of these rates were just adjusted downward by the Tax Cuts and Jobs Act of 2017. The reduction in rates became effective with the 2018 calendar year. A reduction in personal income taxes was a prominent feature of Donald Trump's election campaign in 2016.[1]

If you think this is a lot of your income to send to Washington, remember that it was President Kennedy who cut the top bracket from 91% to 70%, and it was President Ronald Reagan who cut the rates further from 70% to 28%. Presidents George H. W. Bush and Bill Clinton suffered tax-cutting relapses, increasing the top rate to 31.0% and 39.6% respectively. President George W. Bush signed a bill in 2001 that cut the top bracket back to 35%. Then in 2009, President Barack Obama increased the top bracket to 39.6%. And in 2017, as mentioned above, the Trump administration reduced the top bracket to 37.0%.[2]

The idea behind progressive (increasing rates as income increases) income tax rates is that the higher income earners should pay more. Of course, they would pay more anyway even if we had a flat tax—that is, if the rate stayed the same regardless of income. As their income increased, the wealthy would pay more dollars. However, progressive rates mean that higher-income earners pay more-more. They pay not only more dollars but also a higher percentage of their incomes. Some Americans think that Uncle Sam should really "sock it to the rich," but the only problem with this idea is that the rich don't always cooperate. It so happens that when income tax rates get too high, the people subject to these rates modify their behavior. They may work less, look for tax shelters, give money away, cheat on their taxes, and even actually lose money in business activities on purpose. Of course, they will only lose money on purpose if they are having fun in the process, such as participating in a business they really enjoy. To be sure, as the federal government raises taxes on higher incomes, the people who are supposed to pay these higher rates don't just sit there waiting to be plucked like a chicken. They take evasive action with the help of tax accountants, attorneys, and financial advisers. It's actually not that different from a football game. When the offense changes its tactics, the defense adjusts.

Economist Arthur Laffer observed that if the income tax rate was 100%, then tax revenue would, of course, be zero (the Laffer Curve) because no one would bother to go to work. If the tax rate was zero, then tax revenue would be zero because no one (at least that I know) would voluntarily pay income taxes. If these two observations are reasonable, then it follows that somewhere between these two extremes, there is an optimal income tax rate where the tax revenue for the government would be maximized. In other words, tax rates can actually be raised so high that they reduce tax revenue instead of increasing it. It then follows that, particularly at high levels, tax rates can be reduced and total tax revenue could increase. The now famous Laffer Curve that resulted from Laffer's analysis was a significant factor generating momentum for the tax cuts that were initiated during the Reagan administration.[3]

A good example of this principle is the infamous luxury tax on yachts. The 10% tax on these vessels (levied in 1990) was so unpopular that even those who could afford to pay it when purchasing a new yacht rebelled, and an industry was virtually destroyed. The tax was finally repealed, but not before it did a lot of damage to the industry and destroyed a lot of jobs—a classic case of government raising a tax rate but reducing tax revenue.[4]

High income tax rates also encourage tax evasion as well as tax avoidance. Tax avoidance is the legal reduction of taxes through approved deductions. Tax evasion is the illegal avoidance of taxes through not reporting or hiding income. Economies with high income tax rates can generally expect a higher level of tax evasion than if they had lower rates. The reason is that the reward for tax evasion is much higher in a high income tax rate system. One of the best methods of reducing tax evasion is simply to lower income tax rates. This is a simple method of reducing the rewards for illegal behavior. More income tends to be reported, which may maintain or even enhance tax revenue, even at a lower rate.

Progressive income tax rates penalize the creation of additional income in an economy. If those who are upper-income earners are discouraged from working and investing, then the rate of economic growth can be affected. This is one of the great appeals of a flat income tax. A flat tax makes each dollar of income just as valuable as the next. It does not provide the incentives for tax avoidance and tax evasion created by progressive income taxation.

As a general principle, there should never ever be any disincentives for Americans to lawfully make additional income. It is the creative energy of our citizens that generates the standard of living we enjoy today. Economic activity creates the jobs and incomes that make a better life for everyone. We want everyone to work, earn, save, and invest. But we have traveled very far from this concept.

The federal government tax system seems to be designed to penalize the successful, the earning, the senior citizen, the wealthy, the productive, the investor, the innovator, the entrepreneur, and anyone else who is generating income.

What a bankrupt idea. Let's encourage our fellow citizens to do more, to work more, and to invest more. Certainly, the productive and earning should pay taxes for the support of essential services. But some in government seem to believe that the citizen exists primarily to support the government. I don't think this is what the founders of the nation had in mind when they created the United States of America. The second paragraph of the Declaration of Independence reads as follows: "We hold these truths to be self-evident, that all men are created equal, that they are endowed by their Creator with certain unalienable Rights, that among these are Life, Liberty, and the pursuit of Happiness . . . That to secure these rights, Governments are instituted among Men deriving their just powers from the consent of the governed . . ."[5] This makes it clear that the government is designed to serve the people, not the other way around.

With reasonable taxes, the productive will become more productive; and the tax revenue, over the long run, may well be higher, sometimes much higher than it would be with oppressive tax rates. Economic growth will certainly be higher, private employment will be greater, and people will feel more agreeable toward their government. After all, remember, it was a tea tax that helped start the American Revolution in the first place.

A flat income tax is better than a progressive income tax (remember, progressively worse), and a consumption tax is even better. A consumption tax would eliminate all disincentives to work and earn.

The consumption tax, probably in the form of a value-added tax (actually a form of national sales tax), would raise the price of goods purchased in the marketplace. However, it would have the advantage of taxing spending from income, whether earned legally or illegally. April 15 would suddenly be just be another day. There would be no federal tax withheld from your paycheck, and your take-home pay would increase dramatically. The downside would occur when you spent your paycheck and found that prices had increased. The consumption tax would be included in the price of the good on the shelf, as it would be collected from business and industry at each stage of production. The danger is that this tax would simply be added to the existing tax system in order to raise additional government revenue.

The federal tax system we have now is inefficient. Many feel it is generally unfair and that it certainly promotes a lot of tax evasion and tax avoidance. It is time to change it for the better and to destroy its disincentives to work and invest. Let's get rid of the idea of hammering the successful because we are really just zapping ourselves and our economy.

The current federal personal income tax rate reaches 37.0% (reduced in 2017 from 39.6%). When state and local income taxes are included, many US citizens can find themselves at or above a 50% tax bracket, and that rate does not include sales, property, and a host of other taxes paid by citizens. The 37.0% rate amounts to a 32% increase in the maximum income tax rate since the Reagan administration. No wonder American citizens are feeling like they are suffering from taxitis. In addition, many ordinary citizens are making significant federal and state income tax payments although they are barely scraping by while trying to raise a family.

Two significant changes in the current IRS tax code can stimulate increased economic growth and an improved standard of living for citizens. First, the top tax bracket needs to be moved back to the

'80s level of a maximum of 28%, or even 25%. The cut in the top bracket would encourage people in these brackets to reduce their tax avoidance and tax evasion. The 2017 Tax Cuts and Jobs Act doubled the standard deduction for taxpayers from $6,000 to $12,000 and is a family-friendly method of cutting income taxes that has resulted in increasing the take-home pay for millions of working Americans beginning in 2018.[6] With his leadership in passing this act, President Trump has joined President Kennedy and President Reagan as champions of promoting economic growth through tax policy.

However, at this point, you might ask, Well, what about the federal budget? If we cut tax rates and increase deductions, then won't tax revenues for Uncle Sam go down? You would certainly think so. However, we have two examples of what can happen next: the 1960s and the 1980s. Following the 1980s tax cut, federal revenue was down for only one year; and for the 1960s cut, federal revenue never declined. By the time Reagan left office in 1989, total federal revenue was up 51.8%.[7] In other words, many economists believe that these periods document the positive effects of tax cuts on federal revenue. In addition, if these cuts can be coordinated with the careful management of federal government spending, the impact on the federal budget can be minimized. The rate of economic growth during the Reagan years averaged 3.5%.[8]

> *It is important to remember that the goal of the federal government should not be to maximize its revenues, but to maximize the incomes and economic well-being of its citizens.*

I cannot leave a discussion of taxes without dealing with the so misunderstood and so-called capital gains tax. Anytime a politician calls for a cut in this tax, he or she is clobbered for trying to give tax cuts to the rich. Although the top capital gains tax rate is 20%, it continues to be an impediment to economic growth in the US. Some investors may owe an additional Medicare surtax of 3.8% on their gains plus state capital gains taxes, depending on their residency.

Assume, for a moment, that you purchased a home lot ten years ago but have yet to build on it. It has occurred to you to sell it, but you will have a gain on the purchase price of $10,000, which is just enough to account for the rate of inflation over this ten-year period. However, the IRS doesn't care about inflation and will require that you ante up $1,500 in taxes on this property if you are in the 15% capital gains tax bracket. This will leave you with less in purchasing power than you had when you purchased the lot in the first place. Fair? Hardly. But no matter, you had better get your checkbook ready for the folks in Washington. But wait, there is an alternative: don't sell the property. You will not have to pay the tax, the real estate agent will not get the commission, and the government will not get the $1,500. In fact, this very situation occurs all over the US every day. People delay the sale of real estate, stocks, and other capital assets because they believe the capital gains tax is too high and also unfair because it taxes inflation.

In effect, this tax is actually *a capital transaction tax*. Every time you have a transaction with a gain, you have to pay the tax, which tends to reduce the number of transactions. If the tax rate were lower or at least indexed for inflation, the result would surely be an increase in transactions that, even at a lower rate, might increase the level of capital gains tax revenue. In any event, the economy would benefit due to an increase in the number of capital transactions. More real estate would be sold, the number of stock transactions would increase, and the government would collect taxes on most of these events. A 10% tax rate, after indexing for inflation, would have a positive impact on economic activity. Of course, a zero rate would be even better as there would be no impediment to capital flows, which help promote economic expansion.

The estate tax—appropriately called the death tax (because you have to be dead)—is another area of concern for those of us who are worried that federal tax policy can damage economic growth. The estate tax started out at 10% on estates valued at over $50,000 in 1916, but over the years, the rate had increased to 70% by the 1970s. The estate tax personal exemption was raised gradually to $600,000 and the maximum rate reduced from 70% to 55% during the Reagan years. In 2001, under President George W. Bush, the exemption level was raised in stages to $5,000,000 adjusted for inflation.[9] This exemption was doubled under President Trump in 2017 to $10,000,000 adjusted for inflation. Although it was a very significant increase, in my opinion, the tax needs to be eliminated.

This tax is currently assessed upon the death of a single taxpayer with an estate with a value of more than $11,200,000 (2017). The tax begins at 18% and reaches the maximum of 40% with a $1,000,000 taxable estate.[10] Therefore, an individual estate with a taxable base of $20,000,000 would have a potential tax liability of millions of dollars. Particularly if the assets are in the form of farmland, business assets, timberland, and the like, then it is obvious that some or all of the assets may have to be sold to pay the tax. If the assets are primarily in the form of a business, it can easily be seen that the entire business may have to be sold to generate the tax revenue.

This situation can be particularly devastating if the business or farm owner had planned to pass this business down to his or her children. This is the reason that the estate tax or death tax could well be called the anti–small business tax. Remember that General Electric (founded in 1892) never dies. It could go broke, but it never dies. Therefore, it is never subject to the estate/death tax; it just continues as long as it operates effectively. Not so the small or intermediated-sized business, where the owners are the business, which must survive generation after generation of the estate/death tax.

So we knock the little guys back upon the death of the owner but let the big guys roll.

We would never think about assessing the estate/death tax on one of our major corporations every forty years or so. This is because the corporation would be destroyed if they had to convert 40% of their value into cash to pay the tax. The destruction of our most successful corporations makes no sense and would put countless employees out of work. If this is so, then how can it make economic sense to put an estate/death tax on small and intermediate- size businesses? It doesn't! To protect the big corporations from liquidation, the government simply assumes it will never die. Problem solved—at least for the big guys.

This tax is assessed regardless of the ability of the taxpayer to generate the cash to pay the tax. This is why it is so devastating. In addition, a tax rate of 40% really amounts to the confiscation of private property. This is not exactly what the founding fathers had in mind when they set up this country in the first place. Another concern is the tremendous amount of effort that goes into minimizing estate/death taxes each year. The formation of trusts, foundations, and other techniques to try to minimize or avoid the tax takes a tremendous amount of effort and results in the expenditure of a great deal of money. In addition, as already mentioned with regard to the capital gains tax, this tax can cause a lot of decisions to be made that normally would never make sense if the estate/death tax did not exist or was much lower.

The estate/death tax needs to be eliminated. It generates only a small percentage of federal tax revenues but does a lot of damage to small and intermediate-sized businesses. If we are not going to assess this tax on big corporations, how do we justify applying it to small and intermediate-sized businesses upon the death of their owners?

It is time to get practical about federal taxes. Although the 2017 tax act reduced the top bracket from 39.6% to 37.0%, the top bracket is still so high that it interferes with personal decision-making. In addition, the current capital gains tax situation is reducing the number of capital transactions and reducing economic growth. The estate/death tax (although progress is being made) still frustrates the efforts of businesses to survive and prosper. Remember also, the more successful the business is, the less likely it is to survive.

Actually, the most impressive part of the Tax Cuts and Jobs Act is the reduction of the corporate tax rate from 35% to 21%. This is a massive cut and has already unleashed a stream of bonuses, increases in entry-level wages, announced corporate investments, and job increase announcements. In addition, this is the first serious recognition by the US government, in this century, that business tax rates have been seriously out of alignment with the rates in much of the rest of the world economy. Also, those firms organized as sole proprietorships, subchapter S corporations, and partnerships also received a tax reduction. The act provides for a 20% exemption for pass-through income that comes through these organizations. Of course, this does not mean that all this income passes through to the owners as much of the income for this type of enterprise stays in the business to provide for reinvestment in the company.[11]

In addition, corporations have announced that they are going to bring back billions of overseas dollars in reaction to the 15.5% repatriation rate included in the tax act.[12] Apple announced in January of 2018 that it is going to pay $38 billion to the US Treasury in repatriation taxes on overseas cash, expand domestic employment by twenty thousand, and invest $350 billion in the US over the next five years.[13] It seems clear that these business tax reductions are producing and will continue to produce more economic growth across the US economy. It is worth remembering that taxable corporate profits go in only three directions: state and federal income taxes, shareholders, and reinvestment in the enterprise. When corporate taxes are reduced, there is a quick increase in both shareholder value and funds for reinvestment and job creation.

Tax cuts stimulate the economy when the rates are too high and are seriously affecting personal and business decision-making. The swift reaction of business and industry to these corporate rate cuts indicates just how much the higher rates were retarding economic growth in the United States.

CHAPTER 9

What's So Important about
a Central Bank?

While there is no question that presidents and the Congress can have significant positive and negative effects on the long-term economic health of a nation, there is another force that most citizens either ignore or completely misunderstand. The force I am referring to is the Federal Reserve System (the Fed) and the chairman of the board that runs the Fed. Established by the Federal Reserve Act of 1913, the Fed is responsible for maintaining the stability and reliability of the money supply for the United States. Except for some serious miscues (like letting the banking system almost collapse during the 1930s and unleashing galloping inflation during the '70s), there is at least some evidence that the Fed has, to a significant extent, accomplished its mission.

You are already aware (from chapter 4) that the Federal Reserve is directly responsible for the tragedy of the Great Depression. The problem then was too little money. The widespread bank failures of the 1930s, which should have been prevented by the Federal Reserve, destroyed a goodly portion of the nation's money supply and, with it, the fortunes and livelihoods of millions of its citizens. During the depth of the Depression, the unemployment rate reached 25% and the economy was cut in half.[1] In many areas, with virtually no money available, citizens were almost back to the barter system.

Herbert Hoover, president during the early years of the Depression, caught most of the blame, although the Federal Reserve deserves most of the credit. In any event, this economic disaster brought Franklin Roosevelt to the White House and helped create a host of new laws and programs to deal with a depression that should never have happened.

I have frequently told my classes that the government should have printed up a pile of cash, called out the National Guard, told everyone who lost their deposits in a bank to meet down at the courthouse, and handed out the cash. Citizens could have used the cash to save the farm or put food on the table, and the Great Depression would have been cut short. The problem was not too much money; it was not enough. In fact, just dumping money out of airplanes would have been better than the policies the government actually followed during the Depression.

During the Depression, the dollar was king. In fact, the value of the dollar bill actually increased in value during the Depression because price levels fell dramatically due to the low level of economic activity. If you were fortunate enough to have some cash under the mattress or in a bank that did not fail, you were in great shape. You could have bought diamond rings, cars, houses, land, and almost anything else at bargain-basement prices. Many of those who had cash did just that.

My father was off to college during the Depression, and my grandfather (who was a farmer) wrote him a brief note. It said, "Dear Curt, be careful. There is no money." That's just the way it was; there was no money. People who lived through the Depression came out of it with a skeptical eye toward banks and a tendency to save as they had known the hard times and lived to tell about it. From the stories that were related to me growing up, the barter system was alive and well during the Depression. The swapping of mules and farm produce for various other goods and services was what helped many families survive.

The community doctors of the time might not have seen much cash, but they certainly did eat well. This was a difficult time, but there is no question that this experience produced a really tough generation that helped the United States and its allies win World War II.

During the 1970s, it was just the reverse. There was too much money, and the inflation rate soared. I remember that inflation was racing ahead at 1.5% per month in the fall of 1980. It took a big raise for employees just to have a chance of keeping up with inflation, and a trip to the grocery store was a frightening experience. We define inflation as an increase in the general price level of goods and services—or in other words, we were paying a lot more for the same stuff. This inflation (and its far-reaching effects) was a primary reason for the victory of Ronald Reagan over President Jimmy Carter that fall.

The Federal Reserve System had simply let things get out of control. During the Depression, there wasn't enough money; and during the late 1970s, there was too much. The Federal Reserve was set up to prevent this sort of economic destruction. Within a forty-year period, the Federal Reserve had, at one extreme, allowed a third of the banks to fail, ushering in deflation. And then at the other extreme, it allowed galloping inflation to hammer the US economy and its citizens.

So the Federal Reserve System and the way it manages the monetary affairs of the country has had a tremendous impact on the affairs of the nation. Just ask former presidents Herbert Hoover and Jimmy Carter. The Fed can stimulate the growth of the money supply, or it can restrict it using a number of powerful tools at its disposal. The reserve requirements, discount rate, and open market operations are all studied by students of economics on their way to a better understanding of money and economics. Just suffice it to say that if the Fed wants a recession, the economy gets a recession. It may not come off exactly on schedule, but it will happen.

When the economy is overheating and inflation seems to be increasing, you can expect the Fed to boost interest rates and slow the rate of monetary growth. It takes time, and as in the 1981–82 recession, it can be very painful. When the economy is in recession and inflation has finally cooled, you can expect the Fed to lower interest rates and to begin stimulating monetary growth. At the end of the great 1980s expansion, inflation had increased to the 6% range by 1990. The Fed became concerned about this and boosted interest rates and slowed monetary growth. The result was the mild 1990–91 recession. The actual recession was only three quarters long; but as a result, inflation cooled and the Fed began to stimulate the economy again. The recession was actually over in 1991, but the recovery was slow. This slow recovery was an important factor resulting in the failure of President Bush to achieve reelection in 1992. Some of you may remember the theme ("It's the economy, stupid") that Bill Clinton used in his successful campaign.

Although this is a complicated topic, it is important to remember that the Federal Reserve System exerts a tremendous influence on the US economy. Behind the scenes, it is important to determine just what the Federal Reserve is doing and to understand the tremendous influence it has. Its primary mission is to protect the money supply of the nation; and to do this, inflation must remain low. To accomplish low inflation, the Fed must never expand the money supply faster than is necessary for reasonable economic growth. Keep an eye on the Fed, listen to the comments of its chairman, and recognize that the Fed is more powerful than a locomotive. Well, you know the rest.

CHAPTER 10

Take That, You Dirty Rat!

That line, paraphrased from an old gangster movie, is a great opening for one of the most controversial issues of our times: the trade deficit. Each month, as the international trade figures are published, the media trumpets the fact that the US is buying more foreign goods than we are selling (imports are greater than exports). Particularly noted is the sizeable trade deficit with China.

However, we must remember that an important advantage of trading between nations involves the concept of comparative advantage. This encourages each nation to produce what they produce best and then trade with other nations who produce other things best. This means that the total production of all products will be greater worldwide than would be possible if each nation had to be self-sufficient. The net result is that the citizens of the world will have a higher standard of living than would otherwise be possible. An example would be trading petroleum with Japan (they have hardly any, and we have a lot) in return for flat-screen TVs (Japan is really good at producing these). The result is that citizens in both the US and Japan are going to be economically better off.

A tremendous example of a prosperous free-trade zone is the United States. It is a violation of the US Constitution for any of the fifty states to enact tariffs on the imports from any other state in the republic. The result is that merchandise and services flow freely within the nation, our standard of living is high, and the total production of the nation is unequaled. Just imagine what the cost of living in the US would be if every state in the union were able to put tariffs on the goods imported from the other states. Not only would the cost of most everything increase, but the overall standard of living of the nation would be dramatically reduced. The effort by the European Union to provide free trade between its members is exactly what the United States has done for 235 years.

American citizens are often encouraged to believe that the existence of this trade deficit is causing a loss of large numbers of jobs in the US. As a result, various groups frequently encourage Americans to support protective tariffs to protect these jobs. The logic is that these tariffs will prevent as many foreign goods from being imported and, therefore, protect jobs. The problem with this reasoning is that it is we, the American citizens, who have to pay more for imported goods.

Let us say that the US government puts a 20% tariff on foreign-made automobiles, thereby raising the price of these imported cars by approximately this much. Obviously, these car prices must be increased, and it becomes much less likely that they will be purchased. By the way, it doesn't take a rocket scientist to realize that all American auto dealers who are selling Japanese cars are going to be hurt, as well everyone who works for these dealerships. The dockworkers that unload these machines will have less work, as well as the truckers who move them to their destinations.

There is also another effect that is frequently overlooked by the tariff promoters. Tariffs are not paid by foreign producers; they are actually paid by US consumers. These funds flow to the federal government for whatever use they wish and make American consumers poorer by their amount. Foreign producers are, of course, damaged themselves because they can sell fewer cars in the US market, but they do not pay the tariffs. They simply collect them from you and me in the form of higher prices and then forward them to Washington. When the tariff promoters push for tariffs, they frequently forget to tell us that we will be paying the bill or indicate that the price increase won't amount to much. In addition, foreign auto producers will probably agitate with their governments for tariffs on American goods. This will result in higher prices for US goods in these countries. The net result will be that jobs will be lost by US exporters. This can result in a lose-lose situation.

In addition, tariffs on foreign goods are borne more heavily by low-income Americans than by the wealthy. It is not the wealthy who have to skimp to pay for the family SUV and try to keep tennis shoes on the kids. For the wealthy, a tariff can be a minor inconvenience; but for the average American family, anything that raises the cost of living is a real problem.

You may also ask, How is a tariff on the foreign goods going to raise the cost of my American product? Well, if history is any guide, when the competition gets knocked out, the people still in the business will be able to charge higher prices for their products. If we disable foreign competition in automobiles and other products, American producers will no longer be required to be as competitive in either price or quality. In fact, it can be argued that competition from the Japanese automobile industry is the best thing that has happened to the purchasers of automobiles in the US over the past forty years. US auto prices are lower, and quality is higher because of foreign competition. What do you think the quality of American cars would be today if there had been no foreign competition from Japan, Germany, and other countries? You know as well as I do that prices would be higher, and quality would be lower. Our auto industry is much more competitive today than it would have been without foreign competition. There is no substitute for competition to keep us all on our toes and in fighting trim.

But you may ask, What about the effect on American jobs when Americans buy foreign cars instead of American cars? Doesn't this cause a reduction in the total number of jobs in our country and the creation of employment in other countries? Well, it sounds logical, but it isn't. Let's look at the facts. Isn't it interesting that the trade deficit in 2017 reached a record high just as the unemployment rate declined to a record low 4.3%? How can this be if trade deficits destroy American jobs in total? Can it be that the trade deficit sometimes has an almost inverse relationship to the unemployment rate? It has happened before. In the year 2000, the trade deficit broke over $400 billion for the first time as the national unemployment rate declined to 3.9%.[1]

Just what is the explanation for the fact that the large trade deficits of recent years have been frequently accompanied by low national unemployment rates? We must understand that trade deficits can easily be generated when the domestic economy is strong and our fellow Americans are buying everything in sight, including foreign goods. The 1980s through the '90s was a period of strong peacetime economic growth, and during this period, Americans spent a lot of money. We bought a lot of domestically produced goods and services, producing a strong domestic economic expansion that reduced the unemployment rate to one of its lowest rates in thirty years up to that time. However, we also purchased a great quantity of foreign goods that produced large trade deficits at the same time. So if unemployment was at a record low, why all the upset over the trade deficit? Is it justified? In a word, no.

In fact, the best way to get a trade surplus (exports exceeding imports) is to have a good old-fashioned recession—and the longer, the better. In this event, Americans would purchase less, including foreign goods, and the economy would sag, thereby raising the unemployment rate. During the 1981–82 recession, the unemployment rate rose to 10.8% while the trade deficit was small. But who wants a recession? When the expansion started toward the end of 1982, the stock market took off, and the unemployment rate started going down, dropping to 5.2% by 1989. That is just what we wanted: lower unemployment, low inflation, and strong economic growth. And all of this occurred during a period when the merchandise trade deficit was at one of its highest levels in history.[2] The same thing occurred again in the '90s. The unemployment rate dropped lower than in the '80s at the same time that the trade deficit was growing larger.

This does not mean that particular industries can't be hard-hit by the ebbs and flows of international trade. They can indeed suffer employment losses, which can affect the employment of large numbers of workers. However, a productive economy must be dynamic and flexible in order to produce a high standard of living for its citizens. If these losses have been created by the normal economic adjustments in the world economy, we just have to adjust, retrain, and move on. On the other hand, if the losses are the result of unfair trade practices on the part of other nations, then that is an issue that needs to be addressed.

The United States should certainly press for a level playing field in trade. Too often, we have accepted foreign goods freely while the trading country restricts American products. If the whole world were free of trading barriers, the worldwide production of goods and services would be dramatically enhanced. It does seem that much of the rest of the world sees the United States as Daddy Warbucks, and perhaps some of our own actions have contributed to this impression. We should use our immense economic power to negotiate for a reduction of trade barriers on American goods and services. *Fair trade* is a reasonable term to use as long it is not a code word for protectionism. Free trade should be our objective at all times, and we and the world will be better off if we can achieve it.

The upshot of all this is that we need to realize that international trade is beneficial. Protection comes at the expense of the American consumer, who has to pay more, and at the expense of the American economy, which will suffer a reduction in economic growth.

An important area of opportunity in trade is to concentrate on making the business environment in the United States much more attractive for investment and job creation. It seems that almost every action of the federal government in recent years has been in the direction of higher taxes, more mandates, and more regulations. All of this makes it more expensive to do business in the United States. It is certainly a factor in the decision of many corporations to move production and other operations out of the country. Before the 2017 Tax Cuts and Jobs Act, our corporate tax rates were some of the highest in the world, and we seemed to (at least until recently) pass a new regulation every minute. The new tax act has put the United States back into the game and eliminated most of the tax penalty for doing business in America. In addition, the Trump administration has demonstrated a more practical and reasonable attitude toward business regulation. Instead of a hostile government attitude toward business, it is demonstrating a pro-business approach.

One last note. The discussion here has centered on the merchandise (goods) trade deficit. It has not included the total trade picture, which includes the importing and exporting of services. It is here that the US has been very successful. Remember, selling services generates revenue just like selling "stuff" does. We generally run a services surplus by exporting more services to the rest of the world than we import. This is not surprising since the US has been a consistent leader in the service industries.[3]

However, when business, industry, and political leaders, in any country, call for protection against normal foreign competition, or call for a border tax—consumers beware. Your friends from the government are getting ready to put a tax on the things you buy, reduce your selection in the marketplace, damage the economy, and send more of their citizens' money to the central government.

When nations get into trade wars, it is like the citizens of each country taking a hammer, hitting themselves in the head with it, and saying "Take that, you dirty rat."

CHAPTER 11

How Do You Get Economic Growth?

One of the most fascinating topics of discussion among nations, states, and communities is the nature of economic growth. Everybody wants it, and yet there seems to be a consistent disconnect between the desire for growth and an understanding of the factors and conditions that can actually lead to economic growth.

As mentioned in an earlier chapter, someone has to produce something for there to be an advancement in the standard of living. In fact, a whole lot of people have to produce a whole lot of stuff to produce a good standard of living. Without goods and services, we might as well be sitting on a desert island waiting for a coconut to fall out of a tree in order to have something to eat. It's possible that we might get so bored waiting for the coconut to drop that we resort to fishing to have something to do. As soon as we catch the first fish (production), our standard of living will improve. We might even think about climbing the tree to help the coconut down (more production). At this point, we will have gone from a "waiting for a coconut" diet to a coconut-and-fish diet. Now this is progress. The point is someone has to do something that results in production before economic conditions will improve.

When we are faced with hunger and a lack of shelter, production will normally result naturally as we try to survive. Hunting for food, growing stuff, and the construction of some sort of dwelling result from the drive to survive. So there will always be production, but the question is this. How do we encourage the maximization of the production of a given population in order to create a high and growing standard of living?

I have always taught my students in economics that resources are limited but human wants are unlimited. The challenge is to take these limited resources and create the greatest satisfaction of human wants. This involves the efficient employment of available resources to create goods and services that satisfy human wants. We generally refer to these resources as land, labor, management, and capital. It is not only the quantity of these resources that is important but also the quality. Obviously, some labor resources are more productive than others, and some machinery is more capable of producing than other machinery.

Here in the United States, we have moved from the agricultural age to the industrial age and now to the technology age. However, the basics of economic development have not changed. It seems to me that one of the high-value prerequisites for economic growth is an orderly society. It is very hard to work and do business in an environment that is risky and subject to change in a moment's notice. It is difficult to plan, and the risk of loss rises if the rule of law is not in place.

When you look around the world, it is not hard to identify countries where disorder is the rule. Wars, corruption, and political and racial hatreds can be very destructive to the economic process. When you look at these economies, you will generally find a low standard of living and not much prospect for any improvement.

We in the United States have been blessed with a stable political and economic environment for most of our history. The people who immigrated to this country came largely from countries very used to the rule of law. Except for some serious discord during the Revolutionary War and the Civil War, domestic peace has been the order of the day accompanied by a healthy respect for the law by the general population. This fact has worked to our economic advantage and will do the same for any nation.

I can remember my grandfather talking about riding his horse from Magnolia to Junction City back in the day. It was a distance of fifty miles, and he wanted a horse that could make the trip. The roads weren't much in the late 1800s and early 1900s, and government did not have the resources to do much about it. People and materials moved slowly, and the standard of living was modest. I have often said that roads, the military, and the courts and legal system are some of our most valuable government services. There is little disputing that the highway construction during the Roosevelt administration and the Interstate highway system initiated during the Eisenhower administration were some of the best government investments ever.

Governments that provide essential infrastructure investments set the stage for economic development. It has to be the right type of infrastructure and influenced as little as possible by the type of favoritism and graft that seriously seems to infect many governments across the world. All you have to do is take a look at Venezuela to see what happens when order and infrastructure break down.

In fact, it is not too hard to identify that the United States, in recent decades, has neglected its infrastructure while it has tried to solve about every problem known to man. It has let bridges and highways crumble as precious tax revenue has been allocated elsewhere. It is time to get our priorities straight and stop trying to solve the problems government can never solve and get back to the things it is really good at doing.

Okay, we have order, and we have infrastructure. What's next? I would like to suggest that it is a free-market pro-enterprise environment. We always heard this refrain: "We need to tax business more. It is worth remembering that a corporation is nothing more than a legal entity. The corporation itself actually consists of the employees, shareholders, and customers." However, if you tax business heavily, the employees will surely earn less over time, the shareholders will have less value in their investment, and the customers will likely pay more. Any dividends paid by American corporations are already taxed twice: once at the corporate level and again when they are paid out to the stockholders. Sole proprietors, partners, and subchapter S shareholders at least only pay once.

Nations with reasonable business taxes and regulations encourage the creation and growth of business enterprises. Those with an antibusiness attitude are really slowly strangling the goose that laid the golden egg. Business seems easy to blame for most everything, and yet it is actually the enterprise that makes the economic world turn. It is also, by far, the primary source of government revenue when its employees are included. An antibusiness approach to economic development will leave billions of dollars of economic growth on the table every year for any nation. You have to let a racehorse run if you expect to win any races. If you put a 200-pound jockey in the saddle and put on double-weight horseshoes, you will only see the backsides of the other competitors in the race. And that will be for race after race after race.

There is another element that seems absolutely critical to the economic advancement of a nation, and that is quality education. The world is alive with innovation and advancement in fields we did not know existed only a few years ago. Our educational system must keep up and move briskly ahead. Developing nations are gaining ground, and we are not doing so well. The National Assessment of Education Progress has documented that at the twelfth-grade level, only 37% of students were proficient in reading, with lower percentages proficient in mathematics and science. At many colleges and universities, large numbers of entering students cannot demonstrate minimum competencies in reading, writing, and arithmetic.[1]

There is a growing concern among parents about educational results in the US.[2] However, the tendency of government is to respond to these problems with more rules and regulations that, in many cases, only make matters worse. Putting the schools back in the hands of the parents, school boards, administrators, the faculty, and the marketplace is an important step in making sure that our schools can meet the challenges of the future.

There are so many talented teachers and administrators in our public and private schools, and they need the freedom to use these talents in creative and innovative ways to inspire their students. Rule upon rule and regulation upon regulation can stifle these creative energies and drive talented teachers and potential teachers into other professions.

In discussing education, it is important to realize that it is one of the critical factors in addressing the issue of quality of life. It has so much to do with the attractiveness of a nation, a state, or a city. In addition, quality of life means different things to different people. To one, it is the availability of good highways; to another, the presence of mass transportation; to another, access to restaurants and theaters; and to another, the proximity of outdoor sports, such as hunting, fishing, and hiking. However, each of us knows it when we see it (as it pertains to us), and it certainly has a lot to do with an orderly society, quality infrastructure, good schools, and a vibrant business community.

When some of these building blocks (and in some cases, all) are missing, the city or region sags in spite of our best efforts. As cities and communities, and as a nation, we must pay attention to the basic building blocks for economic growth. There is no free lunch. We have to pay attention to the basics or suffer the results.

There are also a number of other factors that can lead to economic growth. Over the years, towns have sprung up around railroad junctions, river ports, and harbors. Entrepreneurs have had a tremendous impact on various areas of the nation. There is no question that the Sam Waltons and Bill Gateses of the world can create tremendous economic activity simply by locating their operations in certain cities and areas. This should be an encouragement for the US to be sure that entrepreneurship is encouraged and recognized for the tremendous role it plays in economic growth and development.

In addition, the availability of natural resources is like a magnet that attracts economic activity. In my part of the world, the discovery of oil in 1920 set off an economic boom that changed the economic landscape of the region. One of the keys in this arena is how efficiently and effectively the natural resources are developed. We have seen in both Venezuela and Russia (and many other countries) that the existence of large natural resource deposits does not necessarily lead to prosperity, particularly when compared to the United States.

Ross DeVol, a Walton Fellow with the Walton Family Foundation, has created some excellent research for what he has titled *Micropolitan Success Stories from the Heartland.*[3] They list seven attributes related to economic success in smaller communities (10–50,000 in population) as follows:

1. Universities and research institutions
2. Community colleges and workforce development
3. Entrepreneurial awareness, support, and access to early-stage risk capital
4. Diversified and thoughtful strategic economic development planning
5. Manufacturing, logistics / supply chain, and direct foreign investment
6. Technology, professional, scientific, and technical services
7. Quality of place

This publication should be priority reading for anyone interested in economic development, particularly in smaller communities.

We have to start by making sure that the environment for economic development and growth is healthy. Government policies must be examined as to their impact on the economic and competitive environment of a city, a state, or the nation. Too often, we pass laws, rules, regulations, and taxes that seem like a good idea at the time. However, the more the rules, the more the regulations; and the more the taxes, the lesser the activity. Invariably, when you look at an area or nation that is failing to progress economically, you will see that some of the building blocks are in bad shape. So many times in economic development, if we are not careful, we can end up addressing the symptoms rather than the causes.

CHAPTER 12

Have We Discovered the Money Tree?

We in the US used to think that a million dollars was a lot of money. More recently, we have begun to think of a billion dollars in the same way. In addition, we are well on our way to discussing trillions of dollars, particularly when referencing the federal government of the United States.

Just fifteen years ago, the national debt was near $7 trillion; and today (2018), it is in the $20-plus trillion range.[1] This is a massive explosion in the borrowing obligations of whoever is in charge in Washington, DC, at the moment. This is a tripling of the obligations of the federal government and can be described in no other way than cautionary for the future of our nation.

This level of debt currently amounts to approximately $60,000 per person currently living in the United States. For a family of four, it approaches $250,000. In addition, the debt explosion shows little signs of slowing down. All this is unsettling enough without considering that this total does not include all the potential additional obligations the government has assumed for Social Security, Medicaid, Medicare, and other programs.

A good friend of mine, a noted economist, said, "The US is going broke. It is just going to take a long time." The reason that it is going to take a long time is the basic power and strength of the primarily free market economy that is present in the US. However, as you have read in the previous chapters, the continuing trend toward socialism is a threat to this power and productivity.

The biggest problem with the growing debt is that it is a symptom of the uncontrolled expansion of the federal government. If the federal budget were constrained by the revenues generated, at least there would be a limit on spending. With a seemingly unlimited ability to borrow, Washington goes on its merry way each day with little regard for the looming problem it is creating. In addition, the federal government is much larger than it would normally be, which imposes an additional paperwork and regulatory burden on the productive sector of the economy.

I could spend pages and pages discussing this issue, but it will not change the ultimate destination of the United States federal government if we continue business as usual. Fortunately, most of the states have balanced budget requirements that prevent them from borrowing to meet the monthly budget. They can borrow for infrastructure improvements, such as roads and bridges, but the interest and principal repayment must be included in the balanced budgets of their respective states.

Imagine that you knew that you had unlimited borrowing capability and that the debt would never have to be repaid during your lifetime. This would be an attractive magnet for you to enjoy a high level of borrowing and spending so that you could live high on the hog in the present. This is exactly what is happening in Washington, DC. There is no practical limit on spending, so the party rolls on.

At least for the time being, the politicians in the nation's capital have discovered the money tree.

The problem is that the old adage "there ain't no such thing as a free lunch" has not been nullified. Just ask the citizens of Greece. There the chickens have come home to roost, and everyone there is suffering as they try to get their house in order. We in the United States are a long way from where the Greeks are, but we are on the same road, just at a lower milepost number.

Everyone likes to talk about balancing the federal budget, but no one does it. It is just too easy to keep the printing presses going and going and going. It is like the counterfeiter who has produced the perfect bill. He or she will just keep on printing and spending.

One reason it is easy to keep on doing this is that most of the other nations of the world are doing the same thing. I would suspect that we may be looking at a worldwide inflation coming in the future. But again, this is down the road, and politicians are experts at not looking down the road. They are much better at looking at the next election. That is just the nature of the beast.

Society tends to engage in the same sort of pie-in-the-sky borrowing. Just take a look at the student loan situation, where students borrow tens of thousands of dollars, many with little regard to what their future earnings will be or how they might pay down their debt. It is not unusual to see students who have similar financial means but who graduate with dramatically different levels of debt. One student might work hard and skimp to attend a modestly priced university while another maximizes the borrowing to live a good lifestyle while attending an expensive university.

So here it is. The federal government has a credit card with no limit, and the only requirement is that the interest on the debt is paid each month. There is no requirement to reduce the principal, and increasing the principal is no problem at all.

What a prescription for disaster. This gravy train will continue until the interest on the national debt eats so much of the budget that basic programs begin to suffer and lenders become reluctant to buy more government bonds. It will be much easier to control our federal debt expansion now than to wait until later. Remember, balancing the budget simply stops the bleeding; it does not provide for paying down the debt. However, if the debt stops increasing, as the economy grows, it will become less of a problem.

Here are a few suggestions. First, freeze the department budgets of all the cabinet secretaries. Second, ask the secretaries to cut 5% from their budgets for the next year. Third, look for departments that can be disbanded and have the responsibilities and some of the revenues returned to the states. The Department of Education was created during the Carter administration. I am surprised that I was able to receive a decent education without this federal entity. I had to do a double take when I checked the budget for the US Department of Education (2016 budget nearly $77 billion).[2] The product of three public K–12 school systems, I received a great educational start for my life prior to the creation of this department.

Remember the Civil Aeronautics Board?[3] (It was disbanded during the Reagan administration in 1985.) As a result of that action, air travel became more available to ordinary citizens as the cost of air tickets declined dramatically due to increased competition. I remember that we were suddenly able to afford air tickets for my students to attend competitions and conferences rather than endure the long van rides that had previously been necessary.

The final step is to create a pro-growth tax and regulatory environment for business and industry. The faster the economy grows, the faster federal tax revenue will grow. With an economy growing consistently at 3% or better (instead of 1% or 2%), the federal treasury will enjoy excellent cash flow. Taxes are certainly necessary, but when they reduce the incentives to work and invest, economic growth will be reduced. The 2017 Tax Cuts and Jobs Act was a dramatic step toward increasing the level of economic growth and job creation in the United States. The benefits of this act will be far-reaching, and the impact is going to rejuvenate the ability of US businesses to compete in the world market.

However, just like the business and personal tax cuts in 1964 and 1981 and 1986, there is a tendency to revert to higher income taxes and creeping regulation expansion that can erode the ability of businesses to grow and even survive. We must remember that government is supposed to make "life, liberty, and the pursuit of happiness" easier, not more difficult. The government should be the servant of the people and not the other way around.

In addition, isn't it interesting that the federal government wants our banks and businesses to be financially responsible but is much less concerned about the Washington debt machine? In fact, one might legitimately say that the greatest current threat to the future of the government of the United States is a decline in its financial solvency. We currently have almost textbook examples of financial difficulties well represented by the nations of Greece and Venezuela. They are struggling in a sea of socialism and debt and will likely continue to do so.

This reminds us, again, that socialism works. It just doesn't work very well, and it involves a significant loss of individual freedom. Today, I would add that it also has within it the seeds of its own decline.

CHAPTER 13

You've Got to Be Kidding!

The title of this chapter is a not a very unusual reaction to the total of hospital and medical bills in recent years. The story is told of one hospital that had its recovery room next door to the cashier's office. Another describes the medical facility that does a financial analysis on entering patients to determine what illnesses they can afford to have.

Of course, it is no joking matter that medical bills have increased at a hectic pace over the past few years and that American citizens have become more and more concerned about their ability to meet medical expenses. The latest data indicates that almost 18% of the gross domestic product (GDP) of the country is health care. The GDP is the total market value of all goods and services produced in the United States during a year. This means that health care now accounts for over $3,206 billion of our GDP.[1]

This number has frequently been used as a harbinger of doom, as if it is a disaster that we Americans spend heavily on medical care. It is important to remember that although we spend much in this area, we also, according to many, have one of the best medical care systems in the world. It is also important to remember that many US citizens, when they travel abroad, certainly hope they don't get sick on the trip. An important reason is that we feel that we will get better care here.

The US is well known the world over for the quality and innovation of its medical care. Arguments range far and wide about which country has the best health-care system, and you can make your own determination on that issue. It is certain that the US system is far from perfect, but remember to compare the real with the real. Compare our system with the one in other countries and then draw your own conclusions. In how many countries can you get a CAT scan or an MRI within a few minutes of being admitted to a rural hospital? In how many countries—if you are seriously injured in an auto accident—will a helicopter pick you up and, if necessary, whisk you off to a medical center? In what country can you have a heart problem and receive a stent or even open-heart surgery within a few hours?

One of the top economics thinkers of our time is Dr. Thomas Sowell of the Hoover Institution. I would recommend the chapter titled "The Economics of Medical Care" in his book *Applied Economics* (2008). He provides a very interesting comparison of the medical system in the United States with those where the government is in control. This will help you draw your own conclusions about the discussion around the single-payer concept.

Remember to compare the real with the real. When was the last time you had a friend fly off to Europe for surgery? In fact, it is usually the other way around. We have a high-quality comprehensive medical care system. Yes, it is expensive. We Americans value our health and are willing to spend a lot on it. Heroic (and expensive) measures are used daily in the US to save the lives of ordinary citizens—quite a few of which cannot pay for the services they are receiving.

The US medical care system is experiencing serious challenges; but it is not in a crisis. If you want to see a medical system in crisis, just take a trip to the Russian Federation, formerly the Soviet Union. They have a real crisis in medical care. The service is universal, but the quality of care is very low.[2] Medical care needs to be accessible, but it also needs to be of high quality. In many countries, medical care is universally available; but too often, it is of poor quality, frequently because the government has not allocated the necessary resources.

A significant problem with socialized medicine is the rationing of medical care in an effort to control costs. Cost containment can manifest itself in significant wait times for treatment, the lack of treatment for certain maladies, and the lack of freedom in determining who will provide the care and where the care will be provided. You can be sure that these measures will be no more effective here than in other countries. In fact, you can see what it would be like here in the US by reviewing the problems veterans have been experiencing with the Veterans Administration with regard to their medical care. Governments seem to always make more promises than they can keep, and this is certainly true with health care.

The US health-care system is in a state of constant change as it adjusts to the new economic realities of the current medical marketplace. However, this does not mean that the current system has failed. In fact, many of the strains on the system have been produced by Medicare and Medicaid and, most recently, The Patient Protection and Affordable Care Act. These programs have burdened the medical system with costly government regulations and guidelines. It is all too frequent that government interferes with the marketplace, creates problems, and then interferes more to deal with the problems it created in the first place.

In the early '90s, the US flirted with socializing its medical system (Hillary Care) and then backed away as citizens began to realize the implications of such an action. It is good to remember that there is always a trade-off between economic freedom and economic security. As we citizens move more and more in the direction of economic security, we will sacrifice freedom. In medicine, if we want the government to pay all our medical bills, then the government will direct our medical care. They will surely tell us what medical procedures they will allow, how long we can stay in the hospital, and perhaps what hospital we can use or even who our doctor is going to be. As Milton Friedman reminds us, "There is only one alternative to free markets. Force—some people telling other people what to do." That's the way it is: force or freedom.[3]

In 2010, President Obama led a successful effort to pass through Congress (The Affordable Care Act) a law to require health insurance for most citizens of the United States. Individuals with low incomes now qualify for subsidies, which makes the monthly cost of the insurance lower to individuals who qualify. Coverage for dependents was expanded to age 26, and a preexisting condition coverage exclusion was included. There was also a penalty for failure to join the program.[4] It is worth remembering that whenever the government wants to force you to do something in the economic arena, it should raise a caution flag. It is a good indication that many might have made a different decision if they had a choice. This mandate was rescinded by the 2017 Tax Cuts and Jobs Act.

The objective of the ACA was to increase the number of American citizens with health insurance. This was indeed accomplished, but it involved a loss of freedom with regard to health insurance and medical care. Many are concerned that this is a giant step in the direction of complete socialized medicine. In addition, there is no free lunch in health care; as you cover more and more citizens through the health insurance model, many with preexisting conditions, the premium cost rises dramatically. It is also very easy and tempting for politicians to add mandates for various extra coverages, and thus the cost goes up and up with each addition.

As I mentioned earlier, I have reminded my students over the years that socialism does work; it just does not work very well. This is worth repeating. Socialized medicine does work; it just does not work very well. The problem develops when the citizens (in a democracy) vote more benefits for themselves than the economy can support. A review of the recent economic history of Greece will support this reality.[5]

A favorite joke during the days of the USSR was that it was bad to get sick, but it was worse to go to the hospital. It was touted by the communists that all Soviet citizens received medical care provided by the government—it just was not very good. Here in the United States, socialized medicine is not the answer. The marketplace is the answer.

The free market can work in medicine just as it works for other goods and services.

Medical care is a service, and it can be provided in the marketplace. This competition makes providers more efficient in order to stay economically viable. The success of urgent care centers, walk-in clinics, and telemedicine in recent years reinforces the idea that good medical care can be provided by both the public and private sector with excellent efficiency. The level of competition is really the key to efficiency and innovation. In fact, in spite of the presence of the National Health Service in Britain (which provides care for all), 10%–12% of British citizens purchase private health insurance so they can get the care they want in private hospitals rather than relying on the NHS. Much of the reason involves waiting times for specialty care.[6]

One of the biggest and most challenging questions about medical care in the United States is how to lower its cost without sacrificing quality and accessibility. I believe the marketplace has the answer. If you just look at the automobile industry, you will see that American consumers have access to a wide variety of brands of cars from all over the world—and within these brands, there is an extensive variety of vehicles designed for a variety of needs and which are available at many different price levels. Automobiles are extremely important to health and safety, and yet we look to the marketplace to provide the choices we would like to have.

In the same way, the marketplace can and is providing medical care in a wide variety of different ways with many different options. The sky is the limit if we can unshackle the providers to create the options the consumer desires. We must strive to deliver medical care in an efficient and economical manner if we hope to provide all our citizens with the care they need and desire.

Medical care provided by the marketplace can be very inventive. It responds quickly to the needs of the customer, and costs are controlled by the market itself. We spend a lot on our health here in the United States primarily because we value good health. We want top-notch care, and we want it quick and close to home. All of us would like medical care to be less expensive, but we do not want to sacrifice choice, convenience, or quality. A socialized medical system will likely give us less of all three.

It is important to take a moment to look at the confusion surrounding health insurance. Many citizens may not fully understand the concept of insurance as it relates to the health-care industry. Of course, we recognize that if our car is on fire, it is too late to run by the insurance agency to apply for car insurance. Insurance is designed to protect individuals from events that could happen but have not yet occurred. In other words, the insurance company does not know definitely that it will have to pay for a claim from you when you purchase the insurance. In our college statistics classes, we discuss the law of large numbers where, for instance, out of every ten thousand houses, a certain predictable number are likely to be destroyed each year based on experience. In this way, insurance companies can predict their losses and price their policies.

Remember that you are a candidate for property insurance if the loss has not yet occurred and the likelihood of a loss is based on a statistical history of losses for structures of a similar type. How different is the case of an individual who has a preexisting health condition that will most likely result in large medical bills. In other words, the loss is really fairly predictable. This individual will definitely require medical care that is probably going to be expensive. What insurance company is going to want to take on this policy? It is a guaranteed loss. The company knows that it will have to make sizeable payments to a medical provider. Actually, what this person needs is not health insurance but health care. There is a big difference. Health insurance should be for events that could but are not certain to happen. If they are certain to happen, then insurance is not the solution. Some other arrangement should be made to deal with the expected expenditures.

When government forces insurance companies to insure those with preexisting conditions, these predictable losses will have to be passed on to the other policyholders, making their premiums higher. There is no free lunch in health care. Healthy young persons with that first job will find themselves paying higher premiums because the insurance companies are required to make payments for those with large predictable medical expenses.

Companies that have agreed to insure their customers should honor their obligations to cover them if they should develop serious medical conditions later. That is, after all, why we purchase health insurance in the first place—so that we will be protected in the event we fall ill. However, for those with preexisting serious conditions and no insurance, the real answer is not health insurance but health care. Remember that you can get health care without health insurance. You can pay for it out of your own pocket, your employer can pay for it, or the government can pay for it.

The health insurance industry in the US actually does a reasonably good job of providing coverage for Americans (remember to compare the real with the real). However, two problem areas keep cropping up again and again when discussing health care. These two concerns are the portability of insurance coverage and the problem of preexisting conditions. Portability becomes a problem when an employee decides to change jobs but has some sort of preexisting medical condition. There is then the possibility that the new employer's medical insurance company will not want to provide coverage due to the condition. This employee then loses the mobility that would benefit them, and the economy loses the benefits of the rapid reallocation of labor resources.

Citizens who have preexisting conditions but no health insurance need health care. Since their health-care expenditures are going to be large and predictable to a significant extent, a decision could be made to provide health care for these individuals through a special corporation that receives financial assistance from the government. This corporation would charge normal insurance rates, but it would need additional revenues in order to meet expenditures. Those who could not afford insurance under any circumstance would then seek medical attention through existing programs, such as Medicaid or Medicare. The government should pay for the medical expenses that it requires but are not appropriate for the insurance industry. To do otherwise would be to take credit for providing care but to push the cost off to younger healthy individuals who will pay more. Government has a tendency to mandate certain things but then passes the cost off to someone else. This happens with minimum wage legislation, and it is happening in the field of health insurance.

Americans want to help those who need help. However, we do not need to wreck the private insurance market in an effort to accomplish this goal. There always seems to be a tendency for government to try to command the market to do things it is not designed to do. This is exactly what is happening with health insurance. The result is a perversion of the concept of insurance, which is resulting in higher prices for insurance and less freedom in selecting the policy most appropriate for individual citizens.

The additional premium healthy workers have to pay for their policies is actually a federal health-care tax.

The problem of portability was addressed in 1996 with the passage of the Health Insurance Portability and Accountability Act (HIPAA). This act "provides rights and protections for participants and beneficiaries in group health plans."[7] Remember that portability deals with individuals who have been insured in advance of their illness, not those who, for some reason, have not purchased insurance in the first place. In fact, it would actually pay not to buy insurance at all until you became ill if insurance companies are required to sell you a policy no matter what. Of course, this raises the cost of insurance even further.

An important concept in the discussion of health care is the simple but innovative concept of health savings accounts (created in 2003).[8] This is an account that Americans can accumulate to use to pay medical expenses. This account is yours and grows tax-free. It is also a great retirement medical savings account. Each citizen is able to make tax-free contributions to his or her own medical savings account. Each individual or family would then purchase—individually or through his or her employer—a high-deductible health plan (HDHP). The contribution limit for a family in 2017 was $6,750.[9]

HSAs provide an incentive for patients to economize on medical expenses and even to shop around for the most cost-effective treatment. At present, medical consumers have little incentive to pay any attention at all to costs if covered by insurance. What difference does it make about the cost if everything above a deductible or stop-loss is covered? With a health savings account, it would make a difference because we would be spending from our own account. We even might actually ask our physician, how much is this going to cost?

The big benefit would be a much lower premium for a major medical policy as compared to a full-coverage policy. Major medical policies can provide significant savings over standard policies. In addition, once the HSA account has reached a comfortable level, further contributions to it might not be necessary. We would have full coverage for smaller expenses plus major medical, and we would increase market competition and cost consciousness in the medical industry.

An additional issue involves the deductibility of medical expenses for income tax purposes. If the federal government is really concerned about our health, why not allow taxpayers to deduct all non-covered medical expenses? This would include all health insurance premiums, any deductible and co-pays, and any non-covered medications. This would be a real benefit to American taxpayers, and at the same time, this would be an incentive for better health-care behavior by citizens.

Surely, we do not have to respond to every challenge with more government. If we do, we will soon be turning over most of our paychecks and much of our freedom of choice to the federal and state governments. There is a better way. Let us take a good look at how we can harness the power of the market system to provide health care for US citizens that is both excellent and affordable. Remember, socialized medicine does work; but it is likely that it will not provide us with the quality of and accessibility to the health care we desire.

CHAPTER 14

What Are You Thinking About—Retirement?

In earlier agrarian societies where there was not much availability of financial instruments or large government, retirement was not a hot topic of discussion. People wanted to have some children around to take care of them in their old age, and most continued to work as long as they were physically and mentally able. It has only been in recent years—as financial instruments have become more available and modern governments have instituted old-age benefits—that retirement has become such an important public topic. The concept of retirement at seventy years of age was the brainchild of Baron von Bismarck of Germany (1815–1898), who launched the concept of government taking care of people as they grew older. Of course, in those days (1884), not too many were around at that age to be much of an issue. The retirement age was originally set at seventy years of age but was lowered to sixty-five in 1916.[1]

In the United States and much of Europe, governments have taken it upon themselves to attempt to provide income during the later years of life and, in some cases, even are attempting to provide a minimum standard of living for retirees. It is at this point that economic principles begin to conflict with government promises and the grim realities begin to set in.

In the US in 1950, there were approximately sixteen workers supporting each Social Security retiree. Today there are approximately three, and the baby boomers are now retiring in droves. The prospect of what is going to happen as this horde of citizens retires is causing consternation among governmental planners who are beginning to see the financial handwriting on the wall. Government estimates indicate that the Social Security trust fund will be exhausted by the year 2037. This surely means that general federal revenues will have to be diverted to Social Security in order to keep it financially afloat. This does not provide much assurance to those citizens who are just beginning their working lives or will be retiring beyond this year.[2]

At the present time, the federal government can make no guarantee to young workers that these benefits will be available to future retirees without a modification of benefits, large increases in social security taxes, or a very significant infusion of funds from the general federal budget. By the way, social security taxes are already 35% of total federal revenue.[3] Small wonder that confidence in the social security system is low among US taxpayers.[4] The social security system is currently drawing down the social security trust fund. I do tell my students that social security payments of some sort will be made, but there is no way to determine what the value of these payments will be in terms of purchasing power. After all, the US government does have the power to print money.

Another problem with social security is that it can be a bad deal for Americans who put in many years in the workforce and pay a lot into the system. Their return has averaged approximately 2.0%.[5] In a time when the long-run returns on equity investments in the security markets have averaged approximately 8%, it seems that the government is taking advantage of workers to keep its financial ship afloat. The current realization of this fact among citizens is fueling a real look at options with social security so that generations of future Americans will have a more prosperous financial future. A number of proposals would allow taxpayers to designate at least a portion of the 6.2% of their paycheck they pay in social security taxes for investments besides government bonds. We also pay 1.45% in medical taxes, making a total of 7.65%. Remember that business must match the 6.2% citizens pay with another 6.2%. For an individual earning $25,000 per year, the amount available for such an investment is $3,100. Imagine if this $3,100 were invested at 8% annually for forty years, the value of the investment account would be $901,832 in today's dollars. Just consider if this individual had a spouse earning the same amount for the same period. The total family investment would be twice this amount, or $1,803,664. Not bad for a retirement account. The last time I checked, social security did not offer such a deal. In addition, when the social security recipient and spouse dies, the benefits cease with no residual value. If each citizen had their own account, they could leave any balance to their children or to charity.

Of course, you must remember that the investment markets can be risky and that past investment returns may not be as good in the future. However, these rates of return are averages over a long period, and the funds are being invested in the economic system of the United States of America. We would have to all hope that our collective hard work and energy would keep the US a viable economic powerhouse. If this does not happen, it is unlikely that the government of a failing economy would offer much of an alternative.

A reasonable objective for Americans should be to get a better deal from the government. The problem is that the folks in Washington may have good intentions, but they tend to make their decisions and then leave town before the financial chickens come home to roost. The current Congress and president will make certain promises, but it will be a future president and Congress that will make more decisions about your retirement. If the whole system were more personal, some of these decisions would be yours. These decisions would involve when you retire, how much you withdraw from your retirement each year, and what happens to the balance in your retirement account when you die.

So what should be done? The system appears headed for bankruptcy. Of course, it will not actually go bankrupt because the government will find a way to bail it out. However, many citizens have little confidence in the long-term integrity of the system, and the income generated by the system is not providing much in the way of financial security for millions of retiring citizens.[6] It is time to look at some different options that will make financial sense and improve the economic lives of millions of our fellow citizens. In the long run, it will be cheaper to fix the problem now rather than let it run for several more decades and produce a greater disaster. Remember, the social security tax started out at one-quarter of 1%; and as government programs generally do, it has gotten a little out of hand.

I do believe that the federal government will pay social security benefits as long as it (the government) exists. The big question is this: what will these dollars be worth in purchasing power when you, your children, and your grandchildren retire? It is also possible that many retirees who have saved for their retirements could be means-tested out of social security benefits. We can continue to blunder on and just trust the politicians of tomorrow, or we can look at a new direction. This new direction should give you a role to play in your retirement. This is what real freedom is all about.

This brings us to a discussion of private retirement investment accounts. There are really two major categories of plans, and they are a defined benefit plan and a defined contribution plan. Social security is a defined benefit plan. You pay in, and someone else determines how much you can get out and when you can get it out. In other words, it is out of your hands.

The defined benefit plan was very popular during the industrial phase of American economic development after World War II. We were king of the mountain in terms of industrial production, and many companies set up pension plans for their workers. Many Americans have benefitted from these pensions, and state and local governments have also set up defined benefit plans. This is great unless the projections that the benefits are calculated on turn out to be faulty. This has happened for a number of public and private pension plans as the public and private entities have found out that they have taken on more than they can chew. This has produced a movement away from defined benefit plans to defined contribution plans, which takes away the corporate and public liability for retirement benefits.

Defined contribution plans are owned by the employee and not by the company. These plans can be set up by companies and by private and public entities. The gains and losses of the investments belong to the employees. The most popular of these is the 401(k), the 403(b), and several versions of the individual retirement account (IRA). Most of these plans involve a contribution by the employee with, frequently, a match from the employer. These funds go into an investment account each month and are invested based upon the employee's preferences. The account will grow tax-free until retirement and will provide a supplementary amount to what social security will pay.

If your employer has a 401(k) or a 403(b), please participate! In addition, not only should you participate, you should begin now. In addition, you should take full advantage of the match that your employer provides. Do not leave any money on the table. Some employers will offer a graduated scale. For instance, if you contribute 2%, they will match it. If you contribute 4%, they will match it—and so on up to a certain maximum amount. Please match at the maximum amount. However, you may say "I cannot afford it right now." You cannot afford not to get the match! It is going to make a tremendous difference in your retirement down the road. Not matching is like driving down the road and throwing cash out the window.

These accounts grow tax-free, and they can save on income taxes now. Think about it. You save each month on the income taxes you would normally pay and also have an account that will grow tax-free until retirement. In both cases, you are using the taxes you would have paid to invest in your investment account and benefit your retirement prospects in the future. We are having middle- and lower-income workers retiring today with a million dollars or more in their retirement accounts because they have taken advantage of the employer matches over the years. This account is yours. You can draw on it during retirement, and you can leave the balance to your children or a charity when you die.

You will have a number of possibilities for drawing on your retirement when you retire. The method you choose will depend upon your particular situation. Again, it is important to obtain competent advice. The retirement plan personnel will normally provide investment help and advice as part of the financial services they offer.

If Social Security blunders on, you will surely want to have an opportunity to accumulate a private retirement account. If you are self-employed, contribute to an IRA or look at some of the self-employment retirement account options. Do not wait. The earlier you start, the more beneficial your efforts will be. Get sound advice and move ahead to a better financial future.

There are no guarantees, and we all take our chances in this life. However, the future will arrive, and it is best to have a plan to meet it. Social security should be part of your plan; but if you can supplement those payments, you will be better off as a result.

CHAPTER 15

The Choice Is Ours!

In recent years in the United States, there has been a phenomenal growth in the idea that we can have things just because we are, not because we are productive. Americans must reestablish the idea that in order to have, we must produce.

> *No society can prosper if production is not the primary theme that runs through society and economy.*

Frederic Bastiat—French economist, statesman, and author—wrote *The Law* during the period of the French Revolution in 1848. During a time when France was rapidly turning to socialism, Bastiat wrote:

> Man can live and satisfy his wants only by ceaseless labor; by the ceaseless application of his faculties to natural resources. This process is the origin of property.

> But it is also true that a man may live and satisfy his wants by seizing and consuming the products of the labor of others. This process is the origin of plunder.[1]

Bastiat's brilliant insight makes clear the choices of production or plunder. The production by the individual of goods and services or the use of some means to appropriate the production of others—this is the real economic question. Modern societies have become enamored with the concepts of fairness, equity, living wages, and the general redistribution of income. They and we are losing sight of the role production plays in the whole economic process.

The growth of the socialist state in the United States and other nations is a classic example of the reallocation of the production of millions of hardworking average citizens who rise early each day and try to provide for themselves and their families. They do so by producing goods and services that make life better for both them and all Americans. However, more and more able-bodied working-age citizens are receiving income without producing anything of value for the economy. Either they perform no work at all, or they work at activities that do not result in the production of goods and services or enhance the ability of others to produce. Some actually labor diligently at activities that reduce national production (for instance, creating useless and expensive regulations for the citizen to try to obey). Those who do produce must carry the burden of supporting this growing superstructure of the nonproductive. The result is that the standard of living of ordinary working citizens is not growing as it should.

Add to this the expansion of government interference with business and industry, which increases their costs of operation and makes hiring employees more expensive, and we have the prescription for economic decline. If our government makes getting and keeping a job more difficult and then leaves the average working American with less and less of their paychecks to support his or her family, we are going to have to live with reduced economic expectations for the balance of the twenty-first century.

Freedom has a way of dribbling away a little at a time as we look more and more to government to take care of us and solve our problems. Government always wants more resources, and the more we empower government, the less control we will have over our own lives. Government has an important role to play in any economy. However, as it moves far away from the basic services, eats more of the national income, and interferes more in economic decision-making, national economic decline is not far behind.

However, we do have a choice. We are citizens of a democracy. We can improve our economic future. We have the opportunity to influence our elected representatives and to make changes when necessary. The recent efforts, at the national level, to reduce economic regulation and cut business and personal taxes demonstrate that change is possible. We must all realize just how precious economic freedom is and that socialism is a poor substitute for it. The choice is ours. The consequences of inaction are depressing, but the opportunities for tomorrow are unlimited.

> *When economic freedom is enhanced, personal freedom is enhanced.*
> *When economic freedom is diminished, personal freedom is diminished.*

There will always be those who want to use the coercive power of government to create a socialist utopia that really exists only in their own minds. The only antidote for this is a determination to require a limited economic role for government in order to preserve a free society.

NOTES

Chapter 1

1. Milton Friedman, *Free to Choose* film series, PBS, 1980, Vol. 1.
2. Ludwig von Mises, Preface to the 1962 edition, *Bureaucracy*, New Haven: Yale University Press. 1962.
3. George Orwell, *1984*, New York: Penguin Group Inc. 1950, 2.

Chapter 2

1. Adam Smith, *An Inquiry into the Nature and Causes of the Wealth of Nations*, New York: Oxford University Press, p. 488–489.
2. Fact #915: March 7, 2016 Average Historical Annual Pump Price 1929–2015. United States Office of Energy Efficiency & Renewal Energy, Vehicle Technologies Office. https://www.energy.gov/eere/vehicles/fact-915-march-7-2016-average-historical-annual-gasoline-pump-price-1929-2015.
3. Thomas Jefferson, "First Inaugural Address, March 4, 1801," In *The Papers of Thomas Jefferson, Volume 33: 17 February to 30 April 1801*. Princeton: Princeton University Press, 2006m 145–52.
4. James Gwartney, Robert & Joshua Hall, eds. *Economic Freedom Index of the World, 2017 Annual Report, Executive Summary*. The Cato Institute, 2017.
5. Ronald Reagan, remarks at the Hoover Library, West Branch, Iowa, August 8, 1992.

Chapter 3

1. Thomas Jefferson, *The Declaration of Independence*, July 4, 1776.
2. Milton & Rose Friedman, *Free to Choose; A Personal Statement*, San Diego: Harcourt Brace Jovanovich, 1990, p. 292.

Chapter 4

1. Patrick Henry, *Give Me Liberty or Give Me Death*, St. John's Church, Richmond, Virginia, March 23, 1775.
2. United States Congress. Sixteenth Amendment to the US Constitution. (Passed by Congress on July 2, 1909, and ratified by the states on February 3, 1913). https://www.ourdocuments.gov/doc.php?flash=true&doc=57.
3. *US Federal Individual Income Tax Rates History, 1862–2013*, Washington, DC: The Tax Foundation. https://www.taxfoundation.org.
4. *John F. Kennedy on the Economy & Taxes*, Boston, MA: The John F. Kennedy Presidential Library & Museum. https://www.jfklibrary.org/JFK/JFK-in-History/JFK-on-the-Economy-and-Taxes.aspx.
5. Tim Sablik, "Recession of 1981–82," Federal Reserve Bank of Richmond. November 22, 2013. www.federalreservehistory.org/essays/recession_of_1981_82.
6. United States Congress, HR 4242, *Economic Recovery Tax Act of 1981*, 97th
7. Ronald Reagan, Remarks to State Chairpersons of the National White House Conference on Small Business, DC, August 15, 1986.
8. "Federal Receipts and Outlay Summary," The Tax Policy Center, February 26, 2018. https://www.taxpolicycenter.org.
9. Federal Receipts as a Percent of Gross Domestic Product, Economic research, Federal Reserve Bank of St. Louis, 1930–2016, March 31, 2017. https://fred.stlouisfed.org/series/FYFRGDA188S
10. Ibid.

Chapter 5

1. John Maynard Keynes, *The General Theory of Employment Interest & Money.* United Kingdom: Palgrave Macmillan, 1936.
2. Milton & Rose Friedman, *Free to Choose; A Personal Statement,* San Diego: Harcourt Brace Jovanovich, 1990, p. 292.
3. Walter Williams, *The Murphy Lecture,* Southern Arkansas University, Magnolia, Arkansas: 1983.
4. Henry Hazlitt, *The Wisdom of Henry Hazlitt,* Irvington-on-Hudson, New York: The Foundation for Economic Education, 1993, p. 224.

Chapter 6

1. Thomas Sowell, *Discrimination and Disparities,* Basic Books, New York, 2018, p. 99.

Chapter 7

1. "Employment by Major Industry Category," United States Bureau of Labor Statistics, October 24, 2017, https://www.bls.gov/emp/ep_table_201.htm
2. *"Employment and Unemployment among Youth Summary," United States* Bureau of Labor Statistics, August 16, 2017 https://www.bls.gov/news.release/youth.nr0.htm
3. Billy Graham, "Be Grateful for the Ability to Work," The Kansas City Star, September 4, 2016.

Chapter 8

1. "Notice 1036, Percentage Method Tables for Income Tax Withholdings," United States Department of the Treasury, Internal Revenue Service. January 2018. https://www.irs.gov/irs-pd/n1036.pdf.
2. *US Federal Individual Income Tax Rates History,* 1862–2013, Washington, DC :The Tax Foundation. https://www.taxfoundation.org.

3. "The Laffer Curve," The Laffer Center, https://www. laffercenter.com/the-laffer-center-2/the-laffer-curve/.
4. "Good Riddance to the Luxury Tax," *The Wall Street Journal*, A8, January 6, 2003.
5. United States Congress, *Declaration of Independence*, July 4, 1776. https://www.archives.gov/founding-docs/declaration.
6. *Preliminary Details and Analysis of the Tax Cuts and Jobs Act*, Washington, DC: The Tax Foundation. December 18, 2017. https://www.taxfoundation.org/final-tax-cuts-and-jobs-act. n
7. "Federal Receipt and Outlay Summary," The Tax Policy Center, February 14, 2017. http://www.taxpolicycenter.org.
8. United States Bureau of Economic Analysis, BEA National Economic Accounts, *Current-Dollar and "Real" Gross Domestic Product*, July 27, 2017. https://www.bea.gov/national/ indes.htm.
9. "Federal Estate and Gift Tax Rates, Exemptions and Exclusions, 1916–2014," Tax Foundation, https:// taxfoundation.org/federal-estate-and-gift-tax-rates-exemptions-and-exclusions-1916-2014/
10. United States Internal Revenue Service, *What's New–Estate and Gift Tax, The Tax Cuts & Jobs Act, Pub. 6 No. 115-97, 2018.* https:// www.irs.gov/business/small-business-selfemployment/ whats-new-estate-and-gift-tax.
11. United States Congress. The Tax Cuts and Jobs Act, 2017, Sec. 199A, Qualified Business Income, United States Congress, 115th Cong., 1st sess. Washington, DC. 2017. http://docs. house.gov/billsthisweek/20171218/CRPT-115HRPT-466.pdf.
12. Ibid.
13. Apple Inc., "Apple Accelerates US Investment & Job Creation, "Press Release, January 17, 2018. https://www.apple.com/ newsroom/2018/0.

Chapter 9

1. "Labor Force Employment and Unemployment, 1929–39: Estimating Methods." United States Bureau of Labor Statistics. https://www.bls.gov/opub/mir/1948/article/pdf/labor-force.

Chapter 10

1. "Unemployment Rate 16 Years and Older, 1980–2017." United States Bureau of Labor Statistics. https://data.bls.gov/timeseries/LNS14000000.
2. "US Census Bureau, Economic Indicators Division, US Trade in Goods and Services-Balance of Payments Basis, 1960–2016," United States Census Bureau. https://www.census.gov/foreign-trade/statistics/historical/gands.pdf.
3. 1. Ibid.

Chapter 11

1. "US Student's Academic Achievement Still Lags That of Peers in Many Other Countries," Pew Research Center. http://pewresearch.org/fact-tank/2017/02u-s-students-internationally-math-science/.
2. "National Assessment of Educational Progress, Percentage of Students Performed at or Above Proficient," The Nation's Report Card. https://www.nationsreportcard.gov/.
3. Ross DeVol, *Micropolitan Success Stories from the Heartland*, The Walton Family Foundation, May 2018.

Chapter 12

1. "Historical Debt Outstanding-Annual 2000–2015, Treasury Direct, US Department of the Treasury, https://www.treasurydirect.gov/govt/reports/pd/histdebt/histo5.htm
2. United States Department of Education. *Fiscal Year 2018 Budget, Summary and Background*. 2018. https://www2.ed.gov/about/overview/budget/budget18/summary/18summary.pdf

3. Civil Aeronautics Board, (6/30/1940-1/1/1985), Organization Authority Board, www.catalog.archives.gov

Chapter 13

1. "NHE Summary Expenditures by type of Expenditure and Source of Funds: Calendar Year 2015," United States Centers for Medicare and Medicaid Services, 2015. https://www.cms.gov/Research-Statistics-Data-and-Systems/Statistics-Trends-and-Reports/CMSProgramsStatistics/2015/Downloads/NATL/CPS NATL 2.pdfB

2. Boris A. Rozenfeld, *The Crisis of Russian Health Care and Attempts at Reform*, Santa Monica: Rand Corporation. 1995. https://www.rand.org/plubs/conf proceedings/CF124/CF124.chap5.html.

3. Ibid.

4. "Affordable Care Act – Information for Workers and Families," Employee Benefits Security Administration, Department of Labor. https://www.dol.gov/agencies/ebsa/laws-and-regulations/laws/affordable-care-act/ . . ./co

5. Adam Kindreich, "*The Greek Financial Crisis (2009–2016),*" CFA Institute, July 20, 2017. https://www.econcrises.org/2017/07/20/the-greek-financial-crisis-2009-2016/.

6. Jason Shafrin, "Health Care around the World: Great Britain, *Healthcare Economist,* April 23, 2008. http:/healthcare-economist.com/2008/04/23/health-care-around-the-world-great-britain/.

7. "Health Plans & Benefits: Portability of Health Coverage," United States Department of Labor. https://www.dol.gov/general/topic/health-plans/portability.

8. "Health Savings Accounts (HSA's), United States Department of the Treasury, last modified December 1, 2015. https://www.treasury.gov/resource-center/faqs/Taxes/Pages/Health-Savings-Accounts.aspx.

9. "Health Savings Accounts," United Centers for Medicare and Medicaid Services. https://www.healthcare.gov/glossary/health-savings-account-HSA/.

Chapter 14

1. "Otto von Bismarck, German Chancellor, 1863–1890," United States Social Security Administration. https:www. ssa.gov/history/ottob.html.
2. United States Social Security Administration, "A Summary of the 2017 Annual Reports," *Social Security Bulletin* 70, no. 3 (2010).
3. "Federal Government Receipts & Expenditures," United Bureau of Labor Statistics. https://www.bls.gov/emp/ ep_407.htm.
4. "Do you think Social Security will be able to pay you a benefit when you retire?" Gallup, http://news.gallup.com/poll/1693/ social-security.aspx.
5. Kevin J. Lansing, "Rates of Return from Social Security," Federal Reserve Bank *of San Francisco Economic Letter*, November 12, 1999. https://www.frbsf.economic-research/publications/economic-letter/1999/november/ rates-of-return-from-social-security/.
6. Stephen C. Goss, "The Future Status of the Social Security Program," *Social Security Bulletin*, 70, no. 3 (2010). https:// www.ssa.gov/policy/docs/ssb/v70n3/v70n3p111.html.

Chapter 15

1. Frederick Bastiat, *The Law*, Frederick Bastiat, New York: The Foundation for Economic Education Inc. 1850 (1950 translation). 10.

INDEX

A

air travel, 69
American Revolution, 43
Apple Inc., 49
Applied Economics (Sowell), 72
Aurora (ship), 2

B

baby boomers, 81
banks, 25-26, 32, 51-52, 70
Bastiat, Frederic, 86
Bill of Rights, 15
Bismarck, Otto von, 80
Boston, Massachusetts, 33
bureaucracy, 1, 3, 5
bureaucrats, 2, 13, 15, 21
Bush, George H. W., 24, 41
Bush, George W., 24, 41, 46

C

capital, 8-9, 61
capital gains tax, 45-46, 48
capitalism, 1-2, 6-11, 26, 34
Carter, James Earl, Jr., 8, 22, 52, 69

Cato Institute, 10
China, 5, 54
Civil Aeronautics Board, 69
Civil War, 61
Clinton, William Jefferson, 24, 41, 53
communism, 1-4
competition, 7-9, 56, 59, 69, 75, 79
consumption tax, 43-44

D

Daddy Warbucks, 58
"dead-end" jobs, 35, 37-38
debt, 66-70
    national, 13, 17, 66, 68
Declaration of Independence, vii, 14, 43
defined benefit plan, 83-84
defined contribution plan, 83-84
democracy, 4, 19, 74, 88
DeVol, Ross, 65
discipline, 31, 38
Discrimination and Disparities (Sowell), 33
disincentives, 43-44
dividends, 9, 63

E

economic freedom, 10, 29, 73, 88
Economic Freedom of the World, 10
economic growth, 10, 14, 17, 21-22, 24, 29, 43, 45-46, 49, 53, 57-58, 60-
    61, 63-65, 69
Economic Recovery Act (1981), 22
Eisenhower, Dwight, 62
employment, 26, 28, 32-33, 35-36, 43, 49, 56, 58, 61, 85
entrepreneurs, 7-9, 43, 64
entry-level jobs, 35-38
estate/death tax, 47-48
Europe, 72, 80

European Union, 55

F

fair trade, 58
Fascism, 4
Federal Reserve Act (1913), 50
Federal Reserve System, 20, 25, 50-53
federal revenue, 22-24, 45, 81
First Amendment, 4
Force, 1, 5, 73
foreign goods, 54-58
403(b), 84
401(k), 84
France, 5, 86
freedom, vii, ix, 4, 6-7, 10, 18-19, 21, 24, 32, 64, 73, 79, 87
freedom of enterprise (opportunity cornerstone), 6
"free lunch," 17, 64, 67, 74, 76
free market, 1, 5, 11-12, 14, 73, 75
Free to Choose (Friedman), 14, 26
free trade, 55, 58
Friedman, Milton, ix, 1, 14, 73

G

gasoline, 8
General Electric, 47
General Theory of Employment (Keynes), 26
George III (king), 14
Germany, 56, 80
"Give me liberty, or give me death" (Henry), 19
goods and services, 7-10, 14-15, 39, 52, 57-58, 60-61, 71, 75, 86-87
government, 3-5, 7-33, 36, 38, 41-48, 51, 55-56, 58-59, 62-63, 65-68, 70, 72-74, 76-83, 87-88
  central, 4, 10, 14, 16, 19, 59
  interference, 4-5, 13-14, 19, 73, 87-88
  limited economic role for, 9, 88
Graham, William "Billy," 39

Great Depression, 13, 20, 25-26, 32, 50-52
Greatest Generation, 31
Great Recession, 27
Greece, 5, 67, 70, 74
gross domestic product (GDP), 10, 23-24, 71

H

Hazlitt, Henry, 28
health care, 36, 71-74, 76-79
health insurance, 74, 76-78
Health Insurance Portability and Accountability Act (HIPAA), 78
health savings account (HSA), 79
Henry, Patrick, 19
high-deductible health plan (HDHP), 78
Hillary Care, 73
Hong Kong, 10
Hoover, Herbert, 51-52
Hoover Institution, 72

I

incentives, 7, 25, 27-29, 42, 69, 79
income tax, 17, 20-24, 40-44, 79
    flat, 42-43
    progressive, 42
individual retirement account (IRA), 84-85
inflation, 20-22, 46-47, 52-53
infrastructure, 62, 64, 67
Internal Revenue Service (IRS), 44, 46
"invisible hand," 7
Iran-Iraq War, 8
Italy, 5

J

Japan, 54-56
Jefferson, Thomas, 9, 14
job creation, 9, 49, 58, 69
job experience, 35-38
job opportunities, 34, 36, 38
Johnson, Lyndon, 21
judicial system, 5, 13
Junction City, Arkansas, 30, 62

K

Kennedy, John F., 21, 24, 41, 45
Keynes, John Maynard, 26

L

labor, 8-9, 37, 39, 61, 86-87
land, 8, 51, 61
Law, The (Bastiat), 86
liberty, 15-16, 19, 21, 43, 70

M

management, 45, 61
marketplace, ix, 3, 5, 13, 16, 32, 38, 44, 59, 63, 73-75
Medicaid, 66, 73, 77
Medicare, 45, 66, 73, 77
Micropolitan Success Stories from the Heartland (DeVol), 65
minimum wage, 31-34, 36-38, 78
Mises, Ludwig von, 1
mobility, 17, 77
money tree, 66-67, 69
Moscow, Russia, 2

N

national defense, 14, 21
nationalism, 4
New Zealand, 10
NHS (National Health Service), 75
1984 (Orwell), 4

O

Obama, Barack Hussein, II, 23-24, 41, 74
Obama Care. *See* Patient Care and Affordable Care Act
October Revolution, 2
oil, 8, 64
order, 62
Orwell, George, 4

P

Patient Care and Affordable Care Act, 73
police, 5, 18
portability, 77-78
poverty, 13, 28-29
preexisting conditions, 74, 76-77
price system (operational cornerstone), 7-8
private property, 2, 6, 48
production, 2, 8, 14, 28-29, 44, 58, 60-61, 86-87
profits (entrepreneurial cornerstone), 6, 8-9
public property, 6

R

Reagan, Ronald, 8, 11, 22-24, 41-42, 44-46, 52, 69
Reagan, Ronald Wilson, 22, 24, 45-46, 52
real estate, 46
recession, 22, 27, 53, 57
regulations, 3, 14-15, 17, 21, 29, 36, 38, 58-59, 63-65
resources, natural, 12, 64-65, 86

retirement, 80-85
Revenue Act (1964), 21
Revolutionary War, 61
Roosevelt, Franklin, 25-26, 51, 62
Russian Federation, 72

S

Saint Petersburg, Russia, 2
Singapore, 10
Sixteenth Amendment, 11, 20, 40
skills, job, 30-31, 33
Smith, Adam, 7
socialism, 3, 10, 26, 67, 70, 74, 86, 88
social security, 66, 81-85
Sowell, Thomas, ix, 33, 72
standard of living, 10, 15, 43-44, 54-55, 58, 60-62, 80, 87
student loans, 68
Supreme Court, 40

T

tariffs, 54-56
tax, progressive income, 23, 42-43
taxation, 17, 29, 40-41, 43, 45, 47, 49
tax avoidance, 24, 42, 44-45
Tax Cuts and Jobs Act (2017), 24, 40, 45, 48, 58, 69, 74
tax evasion, 24, 42, 44-45
tax revenue, 3, 41-43, 45, 47
trade deficit, 54-57, 59
trade surplus, 57
trickle-down economics, 23
Trump, Donald, 24, 40-41, 45, 47, 59

U

unemployment, 3, 26, 33, 57
United States, 3, 5, 9-10, 12-13, 15, 25-26, 40, 49-50, 52, 54-55, 58-59,

61-62, 65-72, 74-75, 86-87
US Congress, 20, 50, 74, 82
US Constitution, 4, 9, 15, 20, 32, 40, 54
US Department of Education, 69
USSR (Union of Soviet Socialist Republics, 2-3, 74
US Treasury, 49
utopia, 5, 37, 88

V

value-added tax, 44
Venezuela, 62, 65, 70
Veterans Administration, 73

W

Walton Family Foundation, 65
Washington, DC, 11, 15-16, 20-21, 23-24, 27, 33, 41, 46, 55, 66-67,
    70, 82
Wealth of Nations, The (Smith), 7
White House, 22, 51
Williams, Walter, ix, 27
World War I, 20
World War II, 11, 20, 26, 40, 52, 83